MW01171952

Endorsements

In Prince's book, "Creating Your Encore Career" she takes her years of experience as a career coach and very adeptly shares practical wisdom about how to reimagine what we have traditionally called, "retirement". She allows the reader to envision embarking on a more purpose-driven journey that can be filled with excitement and renewed sense of meaning.

—**Kelley Steven-Waiss**,
Chief Transformation Officer
at ServiceNow and former CHRO

If you're looking for a step-by-step guide to ease you into a purposeful and meaningful retirement, or what Michelle coins your "encore career," look no further! Her clear steps, actionable advice and valuable resources will ensure your transition into your "third" act will be the smoothest one yet. As an executive coach, I highly recommend this book for anyone who is looking to redefine retirement on their own terms.

—**Julia Sorescu**,
founder of GetGritty Coaching & Consulting

Creating Your Encore Career:

A Guide to Finding Purpose and Prosperity in Your "Third" Act

By Dr. Michelle M. Prince

An Encore Career is pursued later in life and is different from one's primary occupation, often being a career shift in lieu of traditional retirement. Creating Your Encore Career covers essential aspects of the Encore Career journey, from self-assessment and career exploration to financial planning, networking, and maintaining work-life balance. The book aims to guide readers to find purpose and prosperity in their 'third act', their Encore Career.

Table of Contents

PREFACE

Inspiration for this book...

In 2011, Jane Fonda addressed a TEDxWomen audience about how we are living on average thirty-four years longer than our great-grandparents. She challenged the audience to think about this increase in longevity and what we wanted to do if we were going to live an extra thirty years. It made me consider how we can re-imagine our work lives, and to ask myself what I would want to do with this new phase of my career (I would have just turned 47 at the time of her live TEDxWomen talk) if I was going to be able to work until well into my 70's. I didn't know it at the time, but this TED talk was an early inspiration for this book.

In 2015, I completed my doctorate in management and organizational leadership, and people in my class, my friends, and my family asked me what I was going to do after graduation. I began to think about what I wanted to do next. I loved the corporate Human Resources and Talent Management leadership work that I was doing. I had already become a certified leadership coach in 2006, and had already spent the better part of twenty years providing internal leadership coaching and creating corporate Learning & Development programs that would benefit employees looking for professional development and leadership development. Inspired by a few very thoughtful and effective leadership coaches in my own circle of colleagues, I decided that I would begin to focus my next career move on coaching to create great leaders. I was fortunate to have the opportunity to just do that on a global scale in my last corporate career role before the start of my Encore Career, and this decision would also set the groundwork of inspiration for this book.

Another inspiration for this book happened in 2018, when I met Lynda Gratton, a faculty member of the corporate executive leadership development program that I was managing at the London Business School. She had just finished writing "The 100-year Life: Living and Working in and Age of Longevity" with Andrew Scott. The premise of this book is that people will be living longer, and therefore we ought to re-think and re-define the traditional education, career, and retirement stages of our lives. The authors claim that due to economic conditions, we need to reconsider finances and retirement schemes, as well as the need to consider multiple career shifts since we'll be living longer, will be in better health, and therefore able to work much longer than our parents and grandparents.

Another inspiration for this book is my personal experience of creating my own Encore Career after experiencing a successful thirty-year career in Human Resources. In 2019, I decided to step out of the corporate work environment and start my own coaching and consulting company. The MPrince Consulting domain was actually established in 2006 when my husband acquired the domain name for me because he said, "One day you are going to go out on your own to do coaching and consulting..." Well, at the end of 2019, I felt like the universe was trying to tell me something. I was nearing the end of a wonderfully incredible three-year international work assignment (my second international assignment in my career) and needed to figure out what I wanted to do next. There were no equitable corporate roles for me where I was working at the time, and I had been with the company six years, so I was okay with looking to make a change.

The most recent and greatest inspiration for this book are the people I know and the clients I have worked with who were brave enough to pursue their Encore Careers.

Introduction

Why choose to make a career transformation?

If you've picked up this book, you may be like many people who are seeking Encore Careers for personal fulfillment and/or financial stability later in life.

Perhaps you've been pursuing a career for ten or fifteen years, or longer, and you are ready to make a change? You feel like you are ready for a career transformation, you know you don't want to keep doing what you've been doing, but you don't know how to get started.

Perhaps you are interested in making a career pivot that might help you regain your enthusiasm for your work? You may have been enjoying the type of work you've done throughout your career, but you are no longer excited for the typical workweek, you are looking for ways to work differently, but you don't know how to get started.

Perhaps you are approaching retirement age and want to start to consider how to make a career pivot? You want to continue to enjoy work and contribute to society, but you would like more flexibility? And perhaps still earn a bit of money while doing it.

Perhaps when you started saving for retirement, you thought about finishing full-time work around age 62, and then playing a lot of golf/tennis/pickleball/_____________ {you can fill in the blank}, or perhaps you dreamt of traveling the world? With changes in retirement benefits and the cost of living continuing to climb, full retirement at age 62, or even age 65, may no longer be feasible. Because people are also living healthier lives longer, you may not be ready to stop working completely. Your retirement savings will likely need to stretch beyond whatever age you had initially planned for as well.

The traditional life framework of *education - career – retirement* may no longer be applicable due to longevity and the changing world. Therefore, in this book we will be considering a new life framework of *education - primary career - Encore Career - full retirement*, and we will refer to your Encore Career as your 'third act'. There have been many inspirations for this book.

As referenced in the Preface, we are living longer, in better health, and like you many people are considering what they want to do as their Encore Career. Everyone's life journey and career decisions are different, and so will your decisions about your Encore Career be unique to you. This book is intended to be inspirational and practical, but it cannot be a one-size-fits-all solution. You need to do the work, and if you need more help, I am available for coaching.

CHAPTER 1
Retirement Redefined?

"The best way to predict the future is to create it."
—Abraham Lincoln

The traditional notion of retirement, where one leaves the workforce entirely at a certain age, is rapidly evolving. This chapter delves into the evolving nature of retirement. We explore how societal expectations of retirement have shifted and discuss the various motivations behind pursuing an Encore Career, such as finding purpose, maintaining social connections, and securing financial well-being.

The Changing Landscape of Retirement Around the World

The changing landscape of retirement and the compelling reasons why individuals are redefining their retirement years are making room for new work models. While some countries still have established statutory retirement ages, most are modifying their pension eligibility and retirement ages due to expected longer working lives.

In 1978, the US Government amended the Age Discrimination in Employment Act (ADEA) to prohibit mandatory retirement before age 70 for the private sector and government jobs. However, forced retirement policies and practices still exist in over 30 US States and in professions that require high levels of physical and mental skill. According to ADP, a payroll and benefits solution provider, some states have begun mandating retirement plans to help address gaps in retirement savings aside from social security (first eligibility at age 65) because research shows that the average working household has virtually no retirement savings. In addition, only four in 10 businesses with less than 100 employees offer retirement benefits (by the way, you may be surprised to hear that 98% of all workers in the U.S. are employed by companies with 100 or fewer employees).

The UK lifted the forced default age of retirement at 65, and now both men and women may work for as long as they decide, with pension eligibility beginning at 66.

In the European Union, the majority of member countries have a legal retirement age between 62 and 67. For example, the statutory retirement age in France is 62, but very soon this will be raised to 64.

Gone are the days when retirement meant leaving the workforce entirely. Instead, people are increasingly looking for ways to stay engaged, find purpose, and secure financial stability in their later years. The changing landscape of retirement is primed for the Encore Career, where individuals use their skills, experience, and passions to embark on a new professional journey while delaying full retirement for a while longer.

In the past, people would retire at a specific age, collect their pension, and enjoy a life of leisure. While this conventional model may still suit some people, it doesn't capture the diverse needs and aspirations of a modern retiree-age person. Today, we find ourselves in an era where the notion of retirement has undergone a transformation reflecting the changing realities of our world, influenced by factors like increased life expectancy, improved health in later years, and a deep desire for personal fulfillment and growth.

People now expect more from their post primary career years, seeking a mix of meaningful activities, ongoing work engagement but with more flexibility, and an opportunity to create more financial security. In addition, the advent of the gig economy and increase in the use of freelancers and independent contractors (called the flexible workforce) have enabled a new type of flexible work arrangement, well suited for those seeking an Encore Career.

The Emerging Encore Career Paradigm

As we've now established, the Encore Career is one that is pursued after your primary career and in lieu of traditional full retirement. Some may refer to it as 'semi-retirement'. Keeping in mind the traditional framework of education - career - retirement, we will consider the new framework of education – primary career - Encore Career - and then full retirement. This is why we refer to your Encore Career as your 'third act'.

You may decide to undertake an Encore Career any time, while this typically occurs between ages 50 to 65. This shift is often characterized by leaving your primary career and embarking on a way to leverage your skills, experience, and passions to contribute to society and find personal fulfillment. Encore Careers encompass a wide range of opportunities from part-time jobs, freelancing, consulting, volunteering, getting on a board, or even starting a business. An Encore Career entails a lifestyle change in that you continue to work and contribute to society, but probably not in the same way you did as a full-time worker.

The Encore Career phase represents a shift in how we approach our post primary career years. It represents the notion that life doesn't stop at a specified retirement age. Instead, we propose that the Encore Career phase is a time for revitalization. A chance for you to explore and find purposeful, engaging work. Here are some key facets of this emerging paradigm:

Increased Life Expectancy: With advances in healthcare and healthier lifestyles, people are living longer. The traditional retirement age may now mark only the midpoint of our lives, offering the opportunity for additional decades of fulfillment in different types of work models.

Desire for Personal Fulfillment: Beyond financial security, individuals are increasingly seeking personal fulfillment and meaning in their post primary career lives. People aspire to leverage their skills, experiences, and passions to contribute to society in a meaningful way.

Ongoing Work Engagement: Instead of disengaging from work entirely, many people wish to remain engaged in activities that bring them joy, stimulate their minds, and make a positive impact. They look for ways to contribute their expertise and experiences, both personally and professionally.

Financial Security: While the focus shifts from a paycheck to personal fulfillment, financial security remains a critical component of the Encore Career paradigm. Economic downturns have unfortunately taken their toll on people's retirement funds and anticipated savings, causing the need for some people to work longer than they expected. Individuals aim to balance their financial needs with their desires for engagement and purpose.

Flexible Options: Encore Careers can take various forms, whether pursuing part-time or flexible work, freelancing, starting a new business, volunteering, or pursuing further education. The path to an Encore Career is as unique as an individual's interests, goals, experiences, and transferable skills.

Lifelong Learning: Encore Careers may inspire learning and applying new ways of working, thinking, collaborating, and delivering support and services. As you enter your Encore Career phase, you may want to acquire new skills and try new ways of learning such as using online learning resources, of which there are many available today. See Chapter 7 for a deeper dive into this topic.

New Aspirations: The Encore Career can also offer the opportunity for exploration and reinvention. Trying out something totally new or joining up with others doing something you've always felt drawn to but never had the time for. From mentorship and advocacy to entrepreneurship and community involvement, there's a wide array of choices to suit different aspirations.

Crafting Your Unique Encore Career

The beauty of the evolving retirement landscape is that it empowers individuals to craft their unique Encore Careers. It invites us to explore our passions, engage with our communities, and embark on a journey of lifelong learning. It is a celebration of the richness of our experiences and the potential we continue to carry into our later years.

As you embark on your Encore Career journey, remember that you have the opportunity to create a legacy, inspire others, create new relationships, and continue evolving. Embrace change, find your balance, maintain well-being, and focus on the fulfillment of your passions and values. Your Encore Career is a testament to the boundless potential for growth, purpose, and joy at any stage of life. May it inspire you and others to embrace your unique third act with open hearts and open minds.

Introducing the Encore Career:
Crafting Your Third Act

This innovative and evolving paradigm represents a third act in your professional journey, a phase of life that begins at the conclusion of your primary career and in lieu of traditional full retirement which may come later. At its core, the Encore Career is marked by a profound commitment to leveraging your hard-earned skills, wealth of experiences, and deeply cherished passions to contribute to society and, more importantly, to find personal fulfillment.

Defining Your Encore Career

An Encore Career doesn't need to be just another job or a simple continuation of work beyond reaching a certain age. It's an opportunity for a transformation of how we perceive and engage with the latter part of our professional lives. It's a deliberate choice to write the next chapter of your career story in a way that resonates with your aspirations and values.

Here are a few elements that may help you consider how to capture the essence of your Encore Career:

<u>Contribution to Society</u>: Through your Encore Career, you can make a meaningful and positive impact on your community by fulfilling a need. You can decide to contribute your skills and expertise where they are needed most, creating value for yourself, your community, and others through the butterfly effect.

<u>Personal Fulfillment</u>: Beyond financial security, an Encore Career is a quest for personal fulfillment. It's about doing work that aligns with your deepest passions, values, and aspirations. It's an avenue for realizing your potential and finding profound satisfaction in your efforts. Your earlier career may or may not have resonated with your passions and values, but your Encore Career should.

<u>Versatility and Variety</u>: Encore Careers may take many forms. The nature of its versatility allows you to tailor your third act to your unique desires and financial situation. Your Encore Career might encompass

a variety of part-time jobs that align with your interests, freelancing or consulting in your area of expertise, volunteering or joining a board, or perhaps venturing into entrepreneurship.

Why the Encore Career Matters

The concept of the Encore Career is integral to our changing landscape of retirement. It recognizes that retirement isn't the end but a beginning, an opportunity for revitalization, exploration, and continued growth. The Encore Career empowers you to fully embrace the vast potential that your wealth of experiences and wisdom brings to the world.

As you stand at the threshold of defining your Encore Career, the canvas is blank, awaiting the strokes of your creativity and the colors of your passions. The pages of your Encore Career story are still being written, and you are the author. You have the opportunity to create a legacy, inspire others, and continue evolving.

The Quest for Purpose

The quest for purpose is an intrinsic part of the human experience. It transcends age and time, and as people live longer and healthier lives, the desire for purpose in later life has gained momentum. Many people who are approaching or have reached retirement age want to stay engaged, give back to their communities, and continue to learn and grow. One of the fundamental pillars of an Encore Career is the opportunity to remain engaged and give back to the community. It's an avenue for individuals to channel their skills and experiences into projects and initiatives that make a significant impact in some way. Whether through mentorship, volunteering, advocacy, or other forms of community involvement, Encore Careers are an active response to the call for purpose.

Retirement doesn't mark the end of one's capacity to learn and grow; as a matter of fact, it can be the beginning of a lifelong learning journey that had to wait until there was time to pursue it. Encore Careers often involve the pursuit of new skills, the exploration of untapped interests, and the discovery of untold passions. This commitment to growth is an essential part of the purpose-driven Encore Career.

The Ongoing Pursuit of Financial Security

Financial security remains a valid concern, particularly in the face of a retirement landscape that has grown increasingly uncertain. Traditional pension systems may not guarantee the financial well-being they once did, there are limitations on government sponsored retirement income, the volatility of investments has had a detrimental effect on many people's retirement savings, and the rising cost of living adds to the worries of people who are reaching or have reached retirement age. Encore Careers can allow individuals to continue earning income, supplementing their savings and pensions, thereby providing an important financial safety net.

If you've not considered retirement savings much or any financial planning up until this point in your life and career, you may be looking at a steeper hill to climb than others who created retirement savings plans earlier, during their primary career. Perhaps preparing for the future may have meant sacrificing the needs you had at the time, so decisions had to be made. No sense in looking back with regret; you cannot change the past. The good news is that it isn't too late to consider ways to bolster your retirement financial stability through an Encore Career. Chapter 6 will go into the Encore Career financial implications more deeply.

Combining Purpose and Financial Stability in Encore Careers

The intersection of purpose and financial stability in Encore Careers is where the true magic happens. Individuals can contribute to society, give back to their communities, and pursue personal fulfillment while also ensuring their financial well-being. This initial focus will help bring a sense of balance and security to the Encore Career journey, reaffirming that it is not just a path to personal fulfillment but also a viable way to safeguard one's financial future.

Let's agree to embrace the potential of Encore Careers as a dynamic, fulfilling, and secure path in the later stages of life. May we inspire you to explore the endless possibilities and embark on your unique Encore Career journey with enthusiasm and confidence.

Personal Advantages of Encore Careers

For individuals considering an Encore Career, the advantages include staying mentally and physically active, building social connections, pursuing passions, and generating additional income. Beyond personal benefits, society at large gains from the experience, knowledge, and expertise that older adults bring to the workforce and the community.

Redefining retirement as the era of Encore Careers brings many advantages, not just for individuals embracing this new paradigm but also for the broader society. Let's explore some of the benefits that accompany this reimagined vision of retirement.

Mental and Physical Activity: One of the foremost benefits of Encore Careers is the opportunity to stay mentally and physically active. Engaging in meaningful work or activities keeps the mind sharp and the body energized. It contributes to a vibrant, healthier, and fulfilling post-career life.

Social Connections: An Encore Career is a social endeavor. It offers the chance to build new social connections and relationships, whether through collaborating with colleagues, delivering to customers, mentoring those in the next generation, or volunteering in the community. These connections enrich one's social circle, contribute to overall well-being, and may further personal longevity.

Pursuing Passions: Many people enter Encore Careers to follow their passions and interests. This is a golden opportunity to delve into hobbies, artistic pursuits, or social causes that may have been on the back burner during your primary career phase along with other obligations such as raising and caring for a young family.

Generating Additional Income: As already mentioned, Encore Careers provide the potential for individuals to continue earning income. This is not just financially beneficial but also adds to one's sense of financial security, which can be especially comforting in the face of a longer life expectancy horizon.

Personal Fulfillment: Perhaps the most profound advantage is the sense of personal fulfillment that comes with aligning one's work with their values, passions, and aspirations. Encore Careers often bring a deep sense of satisfaction, knowing that one is making a meaningful impact in a way that aligns with their values and purpose.

Societal Benefits of Encore Careers

Experience and Expertise: Mature adults bring a wealth of experience, knowledge, and expertise to the workforce and the community. Their wisdom is a valuable resource that can enhance productivity, problem-solving, and innovation in various sectors.

Mentorship and Skill Transfer: Encore Careers offer a platform for mentorship and skill transfer. Mature adults can guide and support the younger workforce, passing on their insights and knowledge, thus nurturing future talent.

Community Engagement: Active engagement in the community is a significant societal benefit. Encore career individuals often have more time to contribute to community development, volunteerism, and social causes, creating a more vibrant and caring society.

Economic Impact: The economic impact of Encore Careers is substantial. The continued earning and spending by mature adults can stimulate local economies and contribute to the financial stability of their community.

Challenging Stereotypes: By redefining retirement, individuals challenge stereotypes about aging and demonstrate that later life can be a time of growth, productivity, and personal fulfillment. This has a profound influence on societal perceptions and expectations.

A Win-Win Proposition

The reimagined retirement, where Encore Careers flourish, is truly a win-win proposition. It empowers individuals to lead lives of purpose, health, and fulfillment while simultaneously benefiting society by harnessing the experience and wisdom of mature adults.

In summary, Chapter 1 has set the stage for us by highlighting the changing nature of retirement. We have introduced the concept of the Encore Career and the motivations for seeking a third act that combines purpose, financial stability, and personal fulfillment. We hope you have gained a clearer understanding of why redefining retirement is a compelling option in today's world. Now, let's dive a bit deeper into your journey.

CHAPTER 2
What do you want to do? Self-Reflection and Assessment

"You don't have to be great to start,
but you have to start to be great." **—Zig Ziglar**

In this chapter, we encourage you to engage in self-reflection and self-assessment as you embark on establishing your Encore Career. By taking the time to explore these elements of your identity, you can gain clarity on what you want to achieve in your third act. We provide guidance on identifying your passions, interests, skills, strengths, values, and priorities. The chapter emphasizes setting personal and professional goals as a foundation for building a successful Encore Career, as these will serve as a roadmap for your Encore Career journey.

The Power of Self-Reflection

This section serves as a compass to help you navigate this introspective self-reflection process, guiding you in discovering your true passions, interests, skills, strengths, values, and priorities. Like many people, you may have never even considered these during your primary career. You may have pursued what you thought (in your late teens/early 20s) what you wanted to '*be*', and you may have pictured what you thought your career would look like. Perhaps you may have even been following someone else's expectations or advice about the type of work you would pursue. Well, now it's your turn to decide what you do next.

Discovering Your Passions: Your passions are the driving force behind your Encore Career. Self-reflection allows you to explore what truly excites you, what activities or causes ignite your enthusiasm, and what you could spend hours doing without feeling like it's work.

Unearthing Your Interests: Interests are the gateways to fulfillment. This chapter helps you delve into the things that pique your curiosity, whether they're long-standing hobbies or newfound fascinations.

Your interests are the threads that can be woven into your Encore Career.

Identifying Your Skills: Your skills are the tools in your career toolbox. Self-assessment helps you identify your competencies, strengths, and areas where you excel. Recognizing your skills is a vital step in aligning your Encore Career with what you're good at.

Understanding Your Values and Priorities

Core Values: Your values are the guiding principles that define who you are and what matters most to you. Self-reflection allows you to identify these values and ensure that your Encore Career aligns with them.

Priorities: Your priorities evolve over time. This chapter assists you in assessing your current life stage, commitments, and responsibilities, helping you set your priorities for this new phase.

Setting Clear Personal and Professional Goals

Goal Setting: Once you've gained clarity on your passions, interests, skills, values, and priorities, it's time to set clear personal and professional goals. This chapter offers guidance on how to create a roadmap for your Encore Career journey, establishing concrete objectives that serve as a guiding light.

Aligning with Your Authentic Self: The self-reflection process ensures that your goals align with your authentic self. It's about designing an Encore Career that resonates with who you are at your core.

Self-reflection and self-assessment are powerful tools for self-discovery. They lead you on a profound journey to understand yourself on a deeper level, revealing your true desires and aspirations. This chapter empowers you to unearth your passions, interests, skills, values, and priorities and set clear goals that align with your authentic self.

If you are having difficulty identifying your passions, interests, skills, values, and / or priorities that's really okay. Give yourself some time to consider them. Go about your day-to-day and take a few notes whenever something comes to mind about it. Perhaps talk with a friend or family member who may be able to help inspire some thoughts about them.

By the time you complete this chapter, you will have a clear understanding of who you are and what you want to achieve in your Encore Career. Armed with this knowledge, you'll be ready to move forward with confidence, knowing that your third act is not just about following a new path but also about embracing the authentic you.

Identifying Your Passions and Interests

The journey begins with a deep exploration of one's passions and interests. What activities make your heart sing? What subjects or causes ignite your enthusiasm? By identifying these core elements, you can uncover what truly motivates and excites you. This self-awareness is a vital foundation for crafting an Encore Career that brings personal fulfillment. This is the pivotal step that sets the stage for an Encore Career brimming with personal fulfillment and authenticity.

Passions: Your Inner Fire

Passions are the inner flames that light up your life. They are the activities, causes, or endeavors that stir your heart, kindle your enthusiasm, and breathe life into your days. Identifying your passions is a key milestone in uncovering your true purpose for your Encore Career. The questions to ask yourself include:

- What activities make you feel truly alive?
- What are you so passionate about that you could immerse yourself in it for hours without feeling like it's work?
- What are the moments in your life when you felt the most exhilarated and fulfilled?

Interests: The Doorways to Fulfillment

Interests are the doorways to fulfillment. They are the subjects, hobbies, or areas of curiosity that pique your interest, fuel your imagination, and encourage your quest for knowledge. Your interests are the threads that can be woven into the tapestry of your Encore Career.

Ask yourself:

- What subjects or topics have always fascinated you, even if you never pursued them professionally?
- Are there hobbies or activities you love to engage in during your free time?
- What new interests have you discovered as you've moved through different life stages?

Creating an Encore Career Aligned with Your Passions

Once you've revealed your passions and interests, the next step is to shape your Encore Career around these core elements. This alignment will foster personal fulfillment and fuel your dedication and commitment to seeing it through. Your Encore Career becomes a reflection of your inner fire and a channel for your interests.

Assessing Your Skills and Strengths

In addition to understanding your passions, assessing your skills and strengths is also an important step. What are you exceptionally good at? What unique talents do you possess? What do people usually seek you out for? Recognizing your competencies allows you to leverage them in your Encore Career. It can also help you identify areas where further development may be necessary to achieve your goals.

In the journey of crafting your Encore Career, understanding your passions and interests is just one part of the equation. To create a truly fulfilling Encore Career, it's imperative to assess your skills and strengths. This chapter is a guide to uncovering your exceptional abilities and talents, which are the building blocks of your Encore Career.

Skills: Your Career Toolbox

Skills are the tools in your career toolbox. They are the competencies you've developed over the years through education, work experience, and personal growth. These skills define what you're exceptionally good at and what sets you apart. The key is to identify these skills and recognize how they can be leveraged in your Encore Career. Consider the following questions:

- What are the skills that you've honed in your professional life?
- In which areas do others often seek your advice or guidance?
- Are there skills you possess that can be applied beyond your primary career?

Strengths: Your Unique Talents

Strengths go beyond skills; they are your unique talents, the qualities that come naturally to you. Strengths are innate, part of your intrinsic makeup. Recognizing your strengths is about embracing the attributes that make you extraordinary. Reflect on the following:

- What are the qualities that friends, family, and colleagues admire in you?
- When do you feel at your best, most authentic self?
- Are there particular areas where you've consistently excelled in your personal or professional life?

Leveraging Your Competencies

Once you've identified your skills and strengths, the next step is to identify ways to further leverage them in your Encore Career. Your skills provide the technical or functional proficiency and expertise you bring to the table, whether it's project management, creative writing, financial analysis, or any other professional area. Your strengths, on the other hand, add a layer of uniqueness and authenticity to your work. They are the qualities that set you apart and contribute to your success.

Identifying Areas for Further Development

While recognizing your competencies is vital, it's also essential to acknowledge where there may be gaps or room for further development - especially if you are going to try something new or unfamiliar for your Encore Career. Perhaps there are new skills to learn or strengths you'd like to enhance in order to achieve your Encore Career goals. Later in this chapter, we provide insights on how to identify and work on these areas for growth and development.

Exploring Your Values and Priorities

Values and priorities play a pivotal role in defining the direction of your Encore Career. What do you hold dear? What are your ethical and moral principles? What are the key elements in your life that take precedence? Understanding your values and priorities helps align your professional pursuits with what matters most to you, ensuring that your Encore Career is personally meaningful.

Values: Your Ethical and Moral Compass

Values are the ethical and moral principles that shape your character and guide your decisions. They are the core beliefs that you hold dear, the principles that define who you are and what you stand for. Identifying your values is an essential step in ensuring that your Encore Career aligns with what matters most to you. Consider these questions:

- What are the principles and beliefs that you uphold in your personal and professional life?
- When you think about your values, what are the qualities and behaviors that resonate with you?
- What are the moments in your life when you felt most aligned with your true self and most authentic to your values?

Priorities: What Takes Precedence in Your Life

Priorities are the key elements in your life that take precedence. They are the responsibilities, commitments, and aspirations that hold special significance. Your priorities can evolve with different life stages, and it's important to assess them in the context of your Encore Career. Ask yourself:

- What is your current life stage and circumstance?
- What are the commitments and responsibilities that are important to you right now?
- What aspirations do you have for this new phase in your life?

Aligning Your Encore Career with Your Values and Priorities

Once you've explored your values and priorities, the next step is to align your Encore Career with them. This alignment is about ensuring that your professional pursuits are in harmony with your core beliefs and the elements in your life that take precedence. Your Encore Career becomes a reflection of your ethical and moral compass, a path that honors what truly matters to you.

Personal Meaning and Fulfillment

Once you have a clear understanding of your values and priorities, you'll be equipped with the knowledge to infuse your Encore Career with personal meaning and fulfillment. Your values and priorities serve as a compass, guiding you in the direction that resonates with your core beliefs and the key elements in your life. This is the magic of purpose-driven self-discovery: it transforms your Encore Career from a mere professional endeavor into a deeply meaningful and personally significant journey.

Need some additional help thinking of what your personal values are? Here is a list of several. Choose up to ten of them, and then rank them to see which ones rise to the top of your list.

Values List

Acceptance	Expertise	Optimism
Achievement	Fairness	Passion
Adventure	Faith	Peace
Authenticity	Fame	Performance
Authority	Family	Play
Autonomy	Freedom	Pleasure
Balance	Fitness	Poise
Beauty	Friendship	Popularity
Being the best	Fun	Power
Belonging	Growth	Productivity
Boldness	Happiness	Recognition
Challenge	Health	Relationships
Citizenship	Honesty	Reliability
Collaboration	Humor	Reputation
Comfort	Independence	Respect
Communication	Influence	Responsibility
Community	Inner Harmony	Security
Compassion	Inspire	Self-Respect
Competency	Integrity	Service
Connection	Intelligence	Spirituality
Contribution	Involvement	Stability
Cooperation	Joy	Success
Courage	Justice	Status
Creativity	Kindness	Support
Curiosity	Knowledge	Teamwork
Determination	Leadership	Time
Discovery	Learning	Trustworthiness
Education	Love	Truth
Empowerment	Loyalty	Variety
Energy	Meaningful Motivation	Wealth
Environment	Openness	Wisdom
		Others not listed

Setting Clear Personal and Professional Goals

Now that you've gained insight into your passions, skills, strengths, values, and priorities, it's time to set clear personal and professional goals. Goals act as a roadmap, guiding your Encore Career journey and helping you stay on track and accountable. In this chapter, we discuss the importance of defining specific, measurable, achievable, relevant, and time-bound (SMART) goals. Whether you're seeking personal satisfaction, financial stability, or both, these goals will help you structure your path, measure your progress, and celebrate accomplishments along the way.

Goals provide a structured framework for your journey. This is important because oftentimes when you are establishing your Encore Career, the only one who is holding you accountable is yourself. Unlike your primary career, where you may have had leaders and managers helping you advance along the way, with your Encore Career you are more likely to be more independent. However, you are not alone. If you need support you can look towards a coach, mentor, trusted friend or relative for support and guidance. These supportive people can also help you hold yourself accountable for the commitments you make as part of your goals.

The Role of Goals in Your Encore Career

Guiding Your Journey: Goals are the guiding lights that lead you through your Encore Career adventure. They provide direction, helping you navigate the vast terrain of possibilities.

Measuring Progress: Goals offer tangible benchmarks for measuring your progress. They enable you to track your development and stay on course. By building milestones for your journey, you will be able to celebrate incremental achievements along the way, if this is something you find motivating.

Ensuring Alignment: Goals help ensure that your Encore Career aligns with your passions, skills, strengths, values, and priorities. They serve as the litmus test for alignment.

The SMART Goal Framework

The SMART framework is a valuable tool for crafting goals that are Specific, Measurable, Achievable, Relevant, and Time-bound. Let's break down what each of these elements means:

- Specific: Each goal should be clear, well-defined, and unambiguous. It should answer the questions "What?" and "Why?"
- Measurable: Your goal should have quantifiable or observable indicators of progress to measure your progress and success. Ideally you can identify incremental steps that are taken in

order to achieve the overall goal. They should provide a way to track your accomplishments along the way and determine when the full goal has been achieved.

- Achievable: While your goal should be ambitious, they should also be attainable. Your goal should challenge you but not be so unrealistic that it feels unattainable, as this can be demotivating.
- Relevant: Your goal should be relevant to your Encore Career and aligned with your passions, skills, strengths, values, and priorities. It should be meaningful in the context of your journey. When you think about your goal, you should feel a sense of excitement about it.
- Time-bound: Your goal should have a defined timeframe whenever possible. Establish a specific date by which it should be achieved or a timeframe in which it could be accomplished. This adds a sense of urgency and commitment.

The magic of goal setting is it transforms your Encore Career from a mere aspiration into a structured and purpose-driven endeavor. This framework also helps you to talk about your ambitions with others, perhaps get their feedback about your plan, and gain their support and encouragement to help you make it a reality.

The Power of Self-Reflection: A Lifelong Journey in Your Encore Career

The power of self-reflection underscores that these are ongoing processes that you'll carry with you throughout your Encore Career journey. This ongoing journey of self-discovery is a dynamic and transformative force that adapts to changing circumstances, remains aligned with your evolving values and interests, and keeps you focused on your goals.

The Continual Process of Self-Reflection

<u>Adapting to Change:</u> Life is dynamic, and circumstances can change. What was once a passion may evolve, or new interests may emerge. Through self-reflection, you can adapt to these changes and ensure that your Encore Career remains in harmony with your authentic self.

Staying Aligned with Values: Your core values remain a compass that guides you your whole life. Self-reflection helps you stay attuned to these values and ensures that your Encore Career is consistent with your ethical and moral compass.

Remaining Focused: The journey to your Encore Career goals is more like a marathon, not a sprint. Self-reflection keeps you grounded and reminds you of your initial aspirations, helping you stay committed and focused on your path.

Measuring Progress: Self-reflection acts as a mirror that allows you to see how far you've come. It helps you gauge your progress, celebrate your achievements, and make adjustments where needed. If you've enlisted the help of others along the way, measuring your progress also enables you to share that accomplishment with others who supported your ability to achieve it.

Embracing the Dynamic Nature of Self-Reflection

I hope you now understand that self-reflection is not just a one-time exercise but a continuous process that adapts to your changing self and circumstances. In doing so, it will keep your Encore Career vibrant, meaningful, and aligned with your true self, throughout your journey and beyond. The exercise of self-reflection can also be useful when things feel less aligned. Examine why - oftentimes it is that you may have strayed too far from your values or priorities. Periodic self-reflection helps you get back on the right path, or it can help you see that a change is needed. Always leave some wiggle room for growth, adaptation, flexibility, and of course the occasional failure - as we are only human. This is the enduring magic of self-reflection: it transforms your Encore Career into a dynamic and evolving adventure of personal growth, learning, and fulfillment.

In summary, Chapter 2 provided a crucial step in the process of creating an Encore Career. We were encouraged to delve deep into our passions, skills, strengths, values, and priorities, providing the necessary self-awareness to chart a course that aligns with our personal and professional aspirations. The emphasis on goal setting ensures that we have a clear and practical roadmap for our Encore Career journey.

CHAPTER 3
What are some of your options? Exploring Encore Career Options

"Dreams are extremely important.
You can't do it unless you imagine it." **—George Lucas**

In this chapter we help you assess which options align best with your goals and interests. One size does not fit all when it comes to Encore Careers. Various paths can shape your Encore Career especially depending on what you want to do. Let's explore your interests, skills, and goals to determine which path aligns best with your aspirations and circumstances.

Whose dream were you following? Maybe in your primary career, you went to school for a certain subject and then went to work based on that area of specialty. Maybe you loved every minute of it, maybe not. But in your Encore Career you are not locked into any specific area of expertise, although you will likely leverage your previous knowledge and experience to benefit your next career move.

Different Encore Career Paths

One of the key messages of this chapter is the sheer diversity of Encore Career options. There is a remarkable tapestry of Encore Career options available, emphasizing the broad diversity that defines this phase of life. There is a vibrant ecosystem where individuals can choose from a multitude of paths, each catering to their unique goals, skills, and interests. Let's dive into the rich array of possibilities, focusing on three general areas including the gig economy, volunteering, and starting your own business.

The Gig Economy: A World of Flexibility and Autonomy

We begin by introducing the gig economy, where individuals can take on freelance, contract, or part-time work, often utilizing their existing skills and expertise. The flexibility and autonomy offered by the gig economy can be highly appealing to those seeking to maintain a work-life balance while contributing to their Encore Careers.

Flexibility: The gig economy provides the freedom to choose when and how much you work. This flexibility is particularly advantageous for those who wish to work as well as enjoy their newfound freedom. Gig work allows you to pursue professional pursuits, but on your terms.

Autonomy: Gig workers have a say in the projects they take on, the clients they work with, and the nature of the work itself. This level of autonomy allows individuals to align their Encore Career with their passions and interests.

Utilizing Existing Skills: Many gig workers leverage their existing skills and expertise, which is a significant benefit. It enables them to contribute to projects that make the most of their experience and knowledge.

If you are thinking about choosing to pursue gig work in your Encore Career, here are a few things to consider:

Self-Assessment and Skill Identification: You've already assessed your skills, strengths, and expertise. Now you can identify the services or solutions you can offer as a gig worker. Consider your professional background and the skills that are in demand in the gig economy.

Define Your Niche: Define a niche within your expertise. Specializing in a specific area can make you more attractive to clients looking for specialized skills. Highlight your unique selling points and what sets you apart from other gig workers.

Legal Structure: Choose a legal structure for your business, such as sole proprietorship, LLC, or corporation. Consult with legal and financial professionals to determine the most suitable structure for your goals.

Insurance: Consider the types of insurance you may need as an independent contractor, such as liability insurance.

Explore Gig Platforms: Research and explore gig platforms that align with your skills. Platforms like Upwork, Fiverr, TaskRabbit, and Freelancer connect gig workers with clients seeking specific services. Understand the types of gigs available, the platform's fee structure, and user reviews.

Create a Strong Online Profile: You will want to craft a compelling online profile that showcases your skills, experience, and expertise. Include a professional photo, write a concise bio, and highlight your accomplishments to stand out to potential clients and customers.

Set Competitive Rates: Research market rates for your services and set competitive pricing. Consider your level of expertise and the value you bring to clients. Be transparent about your rates on your profile and during client interactions. You may need to be flexible in your pricing depending on different customers.

Build a Portfolio: Depending on the type of work you will do, you may need to create a portfolio showcasing your previous work, projects, or achievements. This may include case studies or artistic examples that demonstrate your capabilities. Update your portfolio regularly to reflect your latest and best work. You may want to create an online portfolio that can easily be updated and shared. Sites such as Journo Portfolio, Muck Rack, WordPress, and Dunked all have their pros, cons, and costs, so you'll need to do a bit of research before choosing one.

Create a Website, or Don't: You may want to create a website to convey your services and you can also add financial transactions to some websites. Links to your website can easily be shared via social media or an email link. Sites such as GoDaddy, Weebly, Wix, and WordPress offer easy tools to set up a website, but as with the portfolio sites, they all have their pros, cons, and costs. Do your research before deciding on building a website. Of course, you can also hire someone to build it and maintain it for you, but you'll be the one providing the content. If you will be generating most or all of your work through a gig platform (see above), you may not need your own website at all.

Network and Market Yourself: As a gig worker, you will likely leverage your professional network and some social media to promote your gig services. If you are a professional you likely already have a LinkedIn profile. With your LinkedIn profile you can add a "services page" to highlight what your expertise is as well as receive inquiries directly from interested clients. You can also engage with relevant communities, forums, and online groups to expand your reach and connect with potential clients through LinkedIn and other social media platforms. As you deliver high-quality work and excellent customer service, you will build a positive reputation. Encourage satisfied clients to leave reviews and testimonials on your gig platform profiles.

<u>Diversify Your Skills:</u> Consider expanding your skill set or adapting your expertise to align with emerging trends in the gig economy. Be open to learning new skills that complement your existing ones. To stay updated on industry trends, tools, and best practices relevant to your gig work, participate in online courses, webinars, or workshops to enhance your skills. Highlight how you are staying current on your gig profiles to gain customer attention.

<u>Manage Finances:</u> As a gig worker, you will likely need to keep track of your income, expenses, and taxes. Be sure to fully understand the tax implications of gig work in your location. For example, if you are on contract with a company in the US, they may want to put you on their payroll as a temporary "W2" or ask you to be a "1099" independent contractor. You may want to consider establishing an LLC if you will be doing a lot of independent contractor work. I strongly encourage you to consult with a financial advisor to ensure proper financial management.

<u>Time Management and Organization:</u> As a gig worker, you may have several gigs, several clients, all at the same time. Effectively managing your time is critical to delivering satisfactory work as well as balancing work with other commitments and priorities of your Encore Career. Set realistic deadlines and communicate clearly with clients about project timelines. Check out the many apps available that can provide you with a good time management structure and to keep you organized as well.

<u>Evaluate and Adjust:</u> Regularly evaluate the performance of your gig work. Assess what is working well and where improvements can be

made. Adjust your approach based on the feedback you receive and the evolving gig economy landscape. Also adjust your priorities based on how much work you wish to take on during your Encore Career.

By strategically approaching gig work, you can create a sustainable and fulfilling Encore Career that aligns with your skills, interests, and lifestyle preferences. The gig economy offers a dynamic space for individuals seeking flexibility and autonomy in their professional pursuits during their third act.

Volunteering: Giving Back and Making a Difference

Volunteering is a powerful way to channel your skills, passions, and expertise into meaningful projects. Encore Career individuals often find deep personal fulfillment in giving back to their communities and causes they care about. Volunteering offers a sense of purpose and the opportunity to effect positive change. This is especially true if financial stability is strong and your circumstances and priorities are such where supplemental income is not a concern.

The Rewards of Volunteering

Many individuals are drawn to Encore Careers of volunteerism in the nonprofit sector, leveraging their skills and experience to make a positive impact on society, giving back, and helping others. Volunteering stands as a significant avenue for those considering Encore Careers. It is a path that allows individuals to invest their time, skills, and experience in the nonprofit sector, with the primary aim of making a positive impact on society, seen as a noble endeavor.

<u>Leveraging Skills and Experience:</u> One of the primary attractions of an Encore Career in the nonprofit sector is the opportunity to leverage your existing skills and experience for the greater good. The professional acumen you've honed over your primary career can be channeled into meaningful projects and initiatives. Whether it's providing strategic guidance, financial expertise, marketing skills, or any other area of proficiency, your contribution can be transformative.

<u>Personal Fulfillment Through Giving Back:</u> Volunteering provides a unique avenue for personal fulfillment, often stemming from the act

of giving back to your community or society at large. The rewards of helping others, improving the lives of individuals, or supporting vital causes are immeasurable. As you witness the positive change you bring about through your efforts, a deep sense of gratification washes over you, adding immeasurable value to your Encore Career journey.

Creating a Lasting Legacy: Volunteering in your Encore Career can be more than a personal endeavor; it can be a way to create a lasting legacy. By dedicating your time and expertise to a cause that resonates with you, you leave behind a mark that extends beyond your years. Your contributions become part of a greater whole, impacting communities and generations to come.

A Sense of Purpose: A profound sense of purpose often accompanies volunteering. As an Encore Career volunteer, you are part of something bigger than yourself, contributing to causes that are close to your heart. This sense of purpose can infuse your life with meaning and direction, making each day more fulfilling. The blend of personal fulfillment and the positive impact on society makes this path a compelling choice.

The Ripple Effect of Encore Career Volunteering: Your Encore Career can be a journey of self-discovery and making a meaningful impact on society, leaving a legacy that extends far beyond your own life. This is the profound reward of volunteering as a part of your third act.

If you are thinking about choosing to volunteer in your Encore Career, here are a few things to consider:

Identifying the right volunteer opportunities for your Encore Career involves a thoughtful process that aligns with your skills, interests, and values. Here is some guidance to help you find volunteerism meaningful and fulfilling.

Self-Reflection: Start by reflecting on your passions, skills, and the causes that resonate with you. Consider what skills and expertise you've gained throughout your career, and how they can be valuable assets in the volunteering space.

Identify Causes That Matter to You: Make a list of social, environmental, or community causes that are important to you. Consider issues that ignite your passion and align with your values.

<u>Research Local Organizations:</u> Research local nonprofits, community groups, or NGOs that focus on causes you care about. You may want to attend community events, conferences, or meetings to learn more about organizations operating in your area. Choose groups that allow you to attend a few engagements before fully committing so you can try them out before deciding.

<u>Utilize Volunteer Platforms:</u> Explore online volunteer platforms that connect individuals with organizations seeking volunteers. Websites like VolunteerMatch.org, Idealist.org, Cogenerate.org, and PointsofLight.org provide a database of volunteer opportunities that you can sort through and filter based on your location and interests.

<u>Network Within Your Community:</u> Leverage your existing network and connections to discover local volunteer opportunities. Ask friends, colleagues, or community members for recommendations or introductions to organizations in need of volunteers. Reach out to local community centers, religious institutions, and civic organizations. These entities often have information about volunteer needs and can direct you to relevant opportunities.

<u>Consider Skills-Based Volunteering:</u> Identify opportunities that allow you to leverage your professional skills. Many nonprofits welcome volunteers with expertise in areas such as marketing, finance, technology, or project management.

<u>Attend Volunteer Fairs:</u> Attend local volunteer fairs or community events where organizations showcase their work and volunteer needs. This provides an opportunity to interact directly with representatives from various organizations.

<u>Research the Organization's Impact:</u> Evaluate the impact and effectiveness of the organizations you're interested in. Look for organizations with a clear mission, positive reviews, and measurable outcomes. Contact their volunteer coordinators or managers to discuss your skills, interests, and availability. Ask about ongoing projects, upcoming events, and how you can contribute.

<u>Assess Time Commitment:</u> Ask the organizations what they expect and evaluate how much time you want to realistically commit to volunteering. Be realistic about your availability. Some opportunities may require a few hours a week, while others may involve more

significant time commitments. Consider starting with a short-term or trial volunteer commitment to ensure there is a good fit. This also allows you to assess whether the organization and the role align with your expectations and values.

Stay Open to Change: Be open to exploring different volunteer opportunities if your initial choice doesn't align with your expectations. Volunteering is a dynamic experience, and finding the right fit may require some exploration. You don't have to feel obligated to stay on if the experience is not what aligns with your Encore Career plans and goals.

Remember that volunteering is a two-way street, and finding the right match involves aligning your skills and interests with an organization's mission and needs. By following these steps, you can identify volunteer opportunities that not only contribute to your community but also bring personal fulfillment and purpose to your Encore Career.

Starting Your Own Business

For those with an entrepreneurial spirit, perhaps exploring the option of starting a business sounds exciting. Your Encore Career can take the form of an entrepreneurial venture, allowing you to pursue your passion or create a business aligned with your expertise. This path offers the potential for financial independence and personal satisfaction. Oftentimes, as with gig work, you can set the terms of your business and determine with whom and when you work.

For individuals with an entrepreneurial spirit, starting a business stands as a compelling and transformative option in the landscape of Encore Careers. But starting a business at any stage of your life has its challenges. Do you have what it takes? An entrepreneurial mindset is marked by qualities such as innovation, risk-taking, adaptability, and a strong work ethic. It involves thinking creatively, embracing change, and having the perseverance to overcome challenges.

If you are thinking about choosing to start a business in your Encore Career, here are a few things to consider:

Turn Your Passion and Expertise into a Business: The beauty of starting a business in your Encore Career is that it allows you to turn your passion and expertise into a livelihood. Your business can reflect what truly inspires you. It could be based on a hobby, a creative outlet, a cause you're passionate about, or your years of experience in a specific industry. You may also determine that you can't do it alone or prefer not to, so you may enroll partners to bring your business to fruition.

Market Research: Understanding your niche, or unique value proposition, is a cornerstone of entrepreneurial success. Before launching your business, it's essential to understand your target audience, industry trends, competition, and potential opportunities. Market research provides the insights necessary to shape your business strategy and tailor your products or services to meet the needs of your intended customers.

Create a Business Plan: Business planning is a vital step in transforming your business concept into a reality. The components of a business plan include defining your business's mission and vision, outlining your products or services, strategizing marketing and sales, projecting finances and budgets, and setting operational goals. A well-structured business plan serves as the roadmap that guides your business through its journey. There are many templates available online for creating a business plan.

Do You Need to Secure Financing?: The financial aspect of starting a business may or may not be a significant issue for you, depending on what your business is and how much capital investment is needed for equipment, supplies, etc. It is essential to consider what you will need for startup costs and how you'll fund your venture. There are many different funding options ranging from personal savings, loans, investors, and grants. Securing the needed financing is a pivotal step in ensuring the launch and sustainability of your business.

Legal Structure: Choose a legal structure for your business, such as sole proprietorship, LLC, or corporation. Consult with legal and financial professionals to determine the most suitable structure for your goals.

Business Name and Branding: Choose a business name that is memorable, reflects your brand, and is available for registration. Develop a strong brand identity, including a logo and other visual elements.

Regulatory Compliance: Understand and comply with local, state, and federal regulations and licensing requirements. Obtain the necessary permits and licenses for your industry. If you are unsure of what these requirements are, use the internet to query specifics, and check out sites like the small business association (sba.gov) and SCORE (score.org) that have many resources and templates available to help small businesses succeed.

Insurance: Consider the types of insurance your business may need, such as liability insurance or business property insurance. Insurance protects your business against unexpected events and liabilities.

Technology and Infrastructure: Invest in the technology and infrastructure needed to operate your business efficiently. This may include a website, accounting software, communication tools, and other essential technologies.

Marketing and Sales Strategy: Develop a robust marketing and sales strategy to attract and retain customers. Utilize online and offline channels, social media, and networking to promote your business.

Customer Service and Relationships: Prioritize excellent customer service to build positive relationships with clients. Establish clear communication channels and address customer feedback promptly.

Hiring and Talent Management: If your business requires additional staff, carefully consider the hiring process and talent management. Create a positive work environment that fosters collaboration and productivity.

Adaptability and Learning: Determine how you will stay adaptable and open to learning as your business evolves. Also, determine how you will stay attuned with industry trends, customer preferences, and emerging technologies.

Work-Life Balance: Maintain a healthy work-life balance to prevent burnout. Set boundaries and prioritize self-care to sustain long-term success. Remember, this is your Encore Career, and you are supposed to be enjoying life.

Exit Strategy: Develop an exit strategy that outlines how you will transition out of the business when the time comes. Consider whether you plan to sell the business, pass it on to family member(s), or have other arrangements.

Starting a business in your Encore Career requires careful planning, dedication, and a willingness to adapt. By addressing these considerations, you can lay a strong foundation for a successful and fulfilling entrepreneurial journey in your third act. Whether you're driven by a passion, a lifelong dream, or the desire to create something new, entrepreneurship offers an exciting and transformative option. It's a journey that can infuse your Encore Career with meaning and purpose while allowing you to leave your mark on the world through the business you build.

Do you need to go back to school or acquire new skills?

Education is a lifelong journey, and going back to school is a possibility for those who crave new knowledge and skills. Whether it's pursuing a degree, taking workshops, or enrolling in online courses, going back to school can expand your horizons and equip you with fresh skills for your Encore Career.

Pursuing further education can be a transformative path in your Encore Career. There are many benefits of lifelong learning. Let's explore how to identify relevant skills and knowledge gaps, choose the right educational path, and balance learning with work and personal life during your third act. See Chapter 7 for a deeper dive into this topic.

Evaluating Options Based on Interests and Goals

Aligning your educational choice with your personal interests, skills, and career goals is an important step. It's important to acknowledge that an Encore Career is not a fixed destination; it can evolve and adapt over time. Education is also a lifelong journey, and for those seeking to broaden their horizons and embark on a transformative path in their Encore Careers, pursuing further education and skill-building can be a compelling choice.

Lifelong learning is not just a phrase; it's a philosophy that empowers individuals to expand their knowledge, acquire new skills, and stay current in a rapidly changing world. Here are a few considerations for expanded learning.

Skill Enhancement: Further education enables you to enhance your existing skills and acquire new ones, making you more competitive in the job market or in your chosen Encore Career.

Adaptability: Lifelong learning equips you with the ability to adapt to evolving technologies and industries, ensuring that you remain relevant throughout your career.

Personal Growth: Learning fosters personal growth, stimulates the mind, and broadens your perspective. It's a journey of self-improvement and intellectual enrichment.

There are many educational options available today. Whether you want to pursue online courses, obtain a certification, or enroll in a micro-degree program, there are avenues that cater to different learning styles and goals.

If you are thinking about lifelong learning in your Encore Career, here are a few things to consider:

Identifying Skills and Knowledge Gaps: Before embarking on further education, it's important to identify the skills and knowledge gaps that exist in your chosen Encore Career. Be purposeful and choose to pursue educational options that are going to provide you with the most value and the best outcome towards your Encore Career. Of course, if you simply enjoy learning, then the sky's the limit!

Choosing the Right Educational Path: Consider the relevance of the curriculum, the reputation of the institution, and the flexibility of the program. Consider how you like to learn. Depending on your preferred learning style (for example auditory, visual, verbal, physical, social, self/solo, natural), there are learning options to best suit your preferences. Here are some resources to consider:

Online Courses and MOOCs (Massive Open Online Courses): Many reputable universities and platforms offer online courses that cover a wide range of subjects. Platforms like Coursera, edX, Udemy, and Khan Academy provide access to free or affordable courses. These courses often allow you to learn at your own pace.

Community Colleges and Local Universities: Community colleges often offer affordable courses and degree programs for adult learners. Many traditional universities also have programs specifically designed for older adults.

Scholarships and Financial Aid: There are scholarships and financial aid programs available for older adults who want to pursue further education. These can help offset the costs of tuition and materials.

Senior Discounts: Some educational institutions offer senior discounts on tuition and fees. Be sure to inquire about these discounts when enrolling.

Career Development and Workforce Programs: Many regions have workforce development programs that provide training and education to individuals seeking to transition to new careers. These programs are often tailored to the needs of older workers.

Retirement Communities and Lifelong Learning Institutes: Some retirement communities and lifelong learning institutes provide on-site educational opportunities for residents. These can include classes, workshops, and lectures on a variety of subjects.

Library Resources: Local libraries often provide access to free educational resources, including books, e-books, online databases, and sometimes even classes and workshops.

Professional Organizations: Some professional organizations offer continuing education opportunities and resources for members looking to further their knowledge and skills.

Government Programs: Depending on your location and circumstances, there may be government programs that provide financial assistance or access to education and training.

Online Learning Platforms: Beyond formal courses, there are many online platforms that offer resources for self-directed learning. Websites like Khan Academy, TED, and YouTube have a wealth of educational content.

Educational Apps: There are various educational apps available for smartphones and tablets, covering a wide range of topics. These apps can be a convenient way to learn on the go.

Nonprofit Organizations: Some nonprofit organizations focus on providing education and training to older adults. They may offer resources and support for individuals seeking further education.

Before choosing a resource or program, it's important to assess your specific goals, preferred learning style, and budget. You may also want to consult with an academic advisor or career counselor to help guide your educational decisions. Additionally, consider reaching out to organizations or associations that specialize in the field or subject you're interested in for more tailored advice and opportunities.

Balancing Learning with Work and Personal Life: Balancing education with other commitments, such as work and personal life, can be a challenge. Effective time management and how to strike a balance that ensures you can pursue further education without overwhelming your schedule is certainly something to consider.

Matching Paths to Your Goals and Interests

A key message in this chapter is that one size does not fit all in the world of Encore Careers. Each individual is unique, and the right path is the one that aligns best with your goals and interests. The intent of this chapter was to serve as a guide to help you determine which path resonates most with your passions, skills, goals, aspirations, and circumstances.

In summary, Chapter 3 serves as a comprehensive guide to exploring the various options available in creating an Encore Career. We underscored the uniqueness of each individual's journey and provided practical advice on how to assess and select the path that aligns best with your interests, skills, and aspirations. Whether you are inclined to work in the gig economy, contribute through volunteering, embrace entrepreneurship, or pursue further education, this chapter helps you to make an informed and inspired choice.

CHAPTER 4

What are your concerns? Ageism, Bias, Stereotypes and how to overcome them.

"You may encounter many defeats, but you must not be defeated. In fact, it may be necessary to encounter the defeats, so you can know who you are, what you can rise from, how you can still come out of it."
—Maya Angelou

This next chapter addresses some very real concerns that you may have when pursuing your Encore Career. These include overcoming ageism, avoiding stereotypes, and combating biases. By understanding these challenges, employing strategies to conquer biases, and effectively showcasing the value of your experience, you can navigate the challenges of your Encore Career with confidence and resilience. This chapter will address some heavy issues, but our intent is to empower you with strategies that can help you overcome these challenges - which are very real.

Ageism in the workplace is a challenge many older adults face. It is a real bias that exists and therefore needs to be discussed. However, like all biases and stereotypes, age-related bias can be conquered with the right strategies. We encourage you to not allow ageism to be a significant hurdle for you as you pursue your Encore Career. We emphasize the value of experience and guide you in building a personal brand that defies negative stereotypes.

Overcoming Bias and Ageism in Your Encore Career

Ageism is a form of discrimination based on a person's age, how one thinks about older workers, assumptions they make about older workers, prejudices they feel about older workers, and discriminatory practices and actions taken towards others or oneself based on age.

Ageism can manifest in various ways, from subtle biases to overt discrimination. It can affect hiring decisions, promotions, and overall treatment in the workplace - and it can affect your Encore Career opportunities. Understanding how ageism operates is the first step in effectively conquering it.

In the context of work, ageism often revolves around negative stereotypes, misconceptions, and prejudices related to older workers. These biases can affect how older employees are perceived and treated in various professional settings.

Forms of Ageism in the Workplace and Ways to Overcome Them

Ageism can influence hiring managers to favor younger candidates over older ones. This bias might be rooted in unfounded beliefs that older workers are less adaptable, less tech-savvy, or less energetic. In fact, studies have shown that older workers have stronger work ethic and social skills, are able to learn new technologies when properly trained, and are more mature in their building of professional relationships. Therefore, to combat this, be sure to demonstrate your professionalism and provide examples (i.e. during interviews) of how you have used different technology platforms (either those provided or similar ones). Also, be sure to ask for assistance and training when needed rather than risk making repeated mistakes or errors.

Ageism may impede an older worker's chances of career advancement based on assumptions that they are not interested in climbing the career ladder. Managers may overlook them for promotions or leadership roles based on age-related stereotypes or inaccurate assumptions. Therefore, to combat this, be sure you are clear on your goals and objectives, and clearly communicate these to your management and leadership.

Older employees might be excluded from training and development opportunities under the assumption that they don't need further skills enhancement or are less interested in keeping current with their skills. Therefore, take full advantage of every opportunity to learn, offer to be a reverse mentor to younger workers, volunteer for development opportunities such as new projects and stretch roles. This will help you to overcome any stereotypes that may exist in your workplace.

Negative stereotypes about older workers, such as being resistant to change or lacking in creativity, can lead to unfair treatment and exclusion. Again, the most important technique for overcoming this negative bias is to demonstrate your own change adaptability and your creativity intentionally and whenever possible. Being open-minded, demonstrating a growth mindset, and having a positive attitude will go a long way in ensuring you are included in potential Encore Career opportunities.

Ageism can also marginalize older employees within a workplace, making them feel undervalued and less included in team dynamics. If you are consistently demonstrating willingness to learn, positivity, and resourcefulness, people will want to include you and may even gravitate towards you because you are a strong contributor to building a positive work environment.

Other Strategies and Solutions to Combat Ageism and Stereotypes

We've already provided you with some food-for-thought about how to overcome some of the typical bias and stereotypes in the work environment. Here are a few more things to consider.

<u>Awareness and Self-Advocacy:</u> Know your rights, be able to recognize ageism when it occurs, and advocate for yourself if and when you feel you are experiencing discrimination or bias. It is important to be able to articulate how you are feeling, why you are feeling that way. It is also important to be open to understanding that someone's actions, while affecting you negatively, may have been unintentional. This is called unconscious bias and may occur without the other person realizing what they are doing. By taking the opportunity to raise awareness of the bias, you are helping to remedy the situation for yourself and perhaps for others as well.

<u>Lifelong Learning:</u> We have already emphasized the importance of ongoing skill development and being a lifelong learner. We already provided an extensive list of ways that you can stay current in your field and keep current with the latest technology. Having this growth mindset will enable you to counter common stereotypes of older workers. See Chapter 7 for a deeper dive into this topic.

Building a Support Network: Surround yourself with positive influences and build yourself a supportive group around you as you are establishing your Encore Career. Having a diverse group of people that you can relate to about different challenges and having things in common with them will help you develop your adaptability. In the workplace, identifying peers and mentors who can provide guidance and moral support in navigating workplace challenges is an important aspect to finding joy in continuing to work.

Changing Perceptions, Practical Solutions

By challenging stereotypes, and taking steps to change the perceptions and attitudes that underlie ageism, you are helping to promote diversity, inclusion, and belonging. You are helping to foster a more inclusive workplace environment where age is not a barrier to success for those seeking their Encore Careers. Often referred to as the 'silver workforce', many employers would greatly benefit from considering this valuable pool of talent that continues to grow as the general population continues to age.

Asserting Your Value in the Workplace: Confidence in your abilities is critical when it comes to combating ageism and changing people's perceptions of older workers. We encourage you to go back to the section where you identified your skills, knowledge, passion, and interest to remind yourself of your tremendous value. You are an asset and valuable contributor to the workplace. By consistently demonstrating this value and delivering high-quality work, collaborating effectively with colleagues, and showing your commitment to personal and professional growth, you can help shatter preconceived notions that others may have about older workers.

One of the most potent weapons against ageism is the value of experience. Seasoned workers bring a wealth of knowledge, wisdom, and expertise to the table. Dissuade the assumptions by proactively showcasing your experience as an asset in the workplace. Demonstrate how your past accomplishments and successes can contribute to resolving future challenges and finding innovative solutions. Highlight your flexibility and adaptability. Perhaps offer mentoring or show leadership qualities and professionalism that are often honed through years of work experience. While you are highlighting how your past experience is of value to the people you are working with now, be open to listening and learning from them as well. Everyone adds value in some way - this is key to feeling a sense of belonging.

Fostering Cultural Change: By default, you may become an advocate for a cultural shift in your workplace. By challenging stereotypes and promoting diversity, inclusion and belonging, you can contribute to the dismantling of ageism and other biases, not only for yourself but for colleagues, as well as future generations. By asserting your value and responding proactively to reduce bias and stereotypes, you can in essence disarm intentional and unconscious bias with these actions. By fostering a more inclusive workplace, you may be ensuring that you and others are treated with the dignity and respect deserved - in their Encore Careers and those who are still developing in their careers!

Building a Professional Brand that Defies Stereotypes

If your Encore Career would benefit from you having a professional brand, then this section will be of interest to you. Not only is a professional brand another powerful tool to combat age-related stereotypes, but it can also help you to find work or volunteer opportunities and potential business leads. By creating your own brand you are emphasizing your strengths, expertise, and continued relevance, whereby you are defying any bias that may exist. In today's modern world, building your professional brand that is unique to you personally will likely include creating an online presence that showcases your achievements, enables you to share insights and thought leadership (through posts, blogs, public speaking, etc.) as well as continue to build your professional network with diverse connections as well as others in your field.

The Power of Perception in Your Encore Career

By establishing your professional brand, you are providing others a way to remember you. What do you want to be known for? What impression do you want people to have of you? What do you want people to say about you when you are not in the room? By actively shaping this perception, you can challenge age-related biases and present a strong, dynamic professional image.

Building your professional brand is an ongoing and evolving process. You may wish to monitor and measure the effectiveness of your branding efforts and adapt as needed. Your professional branding should evolve as your Encore Career grows, therefore periodically assessing it and modifying it will keep your brand current and fresh. Here are four key strategies that will keep your personal brand constantly evolving for the better:

<u>Identifying Your Unique Value Proposition (UVP):</u> Your Unique Value Proposition (UVP) is the distinctive combination of qualities, skills, experiences, and passions that sets you apart from others. It's the foundation and consistent messaging upon which your unique professional brand for your Encore Career is built. While it may take some practice, formulating your Encore Career UVP is an important part of creating your professional brand and being able to communicate it to others.

To create your UVP, think about the intersection of your talents, your experience, and your motivators (motivators are your passions, interests, and values). Describe how you intend to use these to serve, to help, to contribute (to people, beings, causes, organization, environment, planet, etc.) As you begin to formulate your UVP, strive to find where there is an overlap between your purpose, passion, and talent. Your UVP will also help reveal the potential Encore Career options that will bring you the greatest sense of joy and fulfillment. Here is a formula that you may find helpful:

> Talent = what you can do
> Passion = what you love to do
> Purpose = what you feel you should do

Your UVP consists of 3 parts:

> What am I meant to do?
> Who am I meant to serve/help?
> What is the result? What value will I create?

Draft your UVP statement (doesn't have to be perfect, and you can continue to evolve it over time).

My purpose (or goal) is to ______________________ (verb/verbs) for _______________________________ (who) to _______________________________ (how I use my strengths) so that ______________________ (difference/impact I make).

Creating an Online Presence: Having an effective professional brand that is unique to you can lead to creating a robust online presence. Depending on what direction you have chosen for your Encore Career, you may be planning to build a professional website or using your LinkedIn profile to showcase your talent and achievements, share testimonials, and demonstrate thought leadership through posts and blogs. LinkedIn also allows you to identify your specific services and explain what you deliver when you establish a 'Services' page as part of your LinkedIn profile, if your Encore Career involves being a freelancer, gig worker, or starting your own business. We'll cover this in greater detail in the next chapter.

Sharing Your Expertise: We encourage you to leverage your knowledge and experience by sharing your expertise. In today's world, this is easier than ever. You can author articles or blog posts, you can create podcasts or be a guest on someone else's podcast, you can speak at conferences - virtual or in person, and of course there is still the option to contribute to industry publications (many have moved to online platforms as well as continuing to offer print versions). These actions highlight your expertise, promote and endorse your business and services, as well as help to challenge age-related stereotypes by demonstrating continued engagement and adaptability.

You may not feel comfortable touting yourself as an expert. That is okay, too. However, by storytelling and being authentic about your professional brand and your UVP, others will benefit. By sharing your journey, your lessons learned, and personal anecdotes not only will you create connection with others, but you will also be an inspiration. If you are not comfortable with storytelling or talking about yourself, that is okay too. This is a skill that can be learned if you become interested in honing this capability. It can also be key to building a strong network of connections.

Effective Networking: These days there is really no excuse for not networking - there are opportunities galore both online and in-person. Building your professional network can help open doors to new opportunities and further establish your professional brand. You can use LinkedIn to network with individuals from all over the world and you can join LinkedIn groups with whom you have a common interest or expertise. Professional organizations offer conferences and events and other social media platforms to connect with others in a professional manner.

If you previously did not build a strong, diverse network of colleagues and connections in your previous work capacity, now is the time to change that. If you only networked with leaders and those above you, what you may find is that the majority of your network has retired and this is why diversity is very important - your network ought to be a collection of people of all ages, stages, and interests. If you were good about maintaining a network of diverse professionals before, that is great because they will become essential to your professional branding and building your Encore Career. We will do a deep dive into Effective Networking in Chapter 5.

By crafting a compelling UVP, aligning your narrative to your professional brand, representing yourself in person and online as experienced in your field, you can build your confidence and empower you to defy preconceived notions about older workers and counter the potential of ageism you may come up against when establishing your Encore Career. Through this well-crafted professional persona, you can challenge stereotypes, create opportunities, and inspire others to recognize and acknowledge the continued relevance and value of older professionals in the workplace.

The Importance of Confidence and Resilience

Next, we will explore ways to bolster your self-confidence, maintain resilience, and embrace the changes and challenges that come with establishing an Encore Career. While creating your Encore Career you may experience some hurdles. Confidence and resilience is key when facing potential ageism and stereotypes. Here are a few strategies for staying positive and focused on your goals in the face of adversity.

Boosting Your Confidence as a Shield Against Ageism

The transformative power of confidence is amazing. Confidence acts as a protective shield against age-related biases and stereotypes by deflecting negativity. When you are self-confident and secure in your abilities and self-worth, you are well equipped to counteract the efforts of anyone or anything that can try to get in your way, including ageism and biases.

Strategies for boosting self-confidence include positive self-talk, visualization, setting and achieving small goals, and practicing self-compassion. Confidence-building exercises such as these can be particularly beneficial whenever entering a new phase in one's career, taking some risks, stepping outside your comfort zone, and engaging in activities to help you establish and grow your Encore Career. Boosting self-confidence in your Encore Career is crucial for navigating challenges and pursuing your goals with enthusiasm. Here are strategies and actions to enhance your self-confidence:

Positive Self-Talk: Replace negative thoughts with positive affirmations. Challenge and reframe any self-limiting beliefs that you may have. Validate assumptions you have that may be creating doubt in your mind. Acknowledge your strengths and past achievements with positivity - validate these with people you trust if you are feeling a sense of self-doubt.

Visualization: Picture yourself succeeding in your Encore Career. Visualize specific scenarios where you confidently gain new business, provide creative solutions, deliver a high level of customer satisfaction, handle challenges, integrate innovation, etc. Use guided imagery to create a positive mental image of your success - however you define success.

Setting and Achieving Small Goals: Break down what may feel like an overwhelming goal into smaller, more manageable actions and tasks. Create a timeline and celebrate your achievements along the way.

This will help to reinforce a sense of accomplishment as you work towards the larger goals, and will strengthen your sense of confidence. *You've got this!* Build momentum by progressively tackling more challenging goals as you feel like you can. Remember, this is your agenda, it's your choice. Adapt your goals to align with your circumstances and your reality as needed.

<u>Practice Self-Compassion:</u> Treat yourself with the same kindness and understanding you would offer to others. Give yourself some grace when needed. Remember, we all make mistakes - these are opportunities to learn and grow and they do not have to be perceived as personal failures. Practice self-compassionate language and avoid harsh self-criticism - tame that inner critic that is always present in the back of your thoughts.

<u>Continuous Learning and Development:</u> By investing in ongoing learning or coaching to enhance your skills and knowledge you will continue to bolster your self-confidence. You can attend workshops, take courses, stay informed about industry trends, and if you need a coach to help guide you and be your 'cheerleader', then hire one! No one said you have to do this all on your own. The more you know, and the better you feel about what you are pursuing, the more confident you'll be.

<u>Networking and Building Relationships:</u> Earlier we touched on the importance of networking for building your professional brand. Connecting with others in your industry or field is also a way to build your confidence. You may find out that you know a lot more than you thought. Networking also provides opportunities to learn from others' experiences and gain insights. Positive interactions with peers and other professionals can certainly act as a confidence booster. If you find yourself feeling less knowledgeable than you thought you were, see the previous paragraph about continuous learning and development.

<u>Accepting Constructive Feedback:</u> Feedback should be perceived as a tool for improvement and it will help you evolve and continue to grow in your Encore Career. While it may be a critique of your abilities, if you view it as constructive criticism and use it to refine your skills,

then you can embrace it as the 'gift' it was intended to be. Embrace a growth mindset that values learning from feedback. Sometimes it may depend on who is providing you with the feedback. This is something to be aware of, and could influence how and whether you accept the feedback.

Physical Health and Well-Being: Prioritizing your physical health through regular exercise, sleep, and a healthy balanced diet can go a long way in developing a positive and confident mindset. Physical well-being positively influences mental well-being. Taking care of your body and feeling well contributes to a more confident mindset.

Appearance and Presentation: How you present yourself will reflect on how others perceive you. First impressions are very important. How do you wish to be perceived? Are you presenting yourself in a way that makes you feel confident? Depending on what your Encore Career is, the type of work environment and customer interaction will likely determine appropriate dress. Our suggestion is to dress professionally and in a manner consistent with your personal style and professional brand.

You don't have to spend a fortune on fancy clothes, and you probably want to look age appropriate but not outdated. At a minimum, shower regularly, brush your hair and teeth, once you are dressed take the time to look at yourself in the mirror using all possible angles. If your hairstyle hasn't changed in over ten years it is probably outdated, consider updating it. If you don't typically wear makeup, consider just adding a light touch of foundation to your daily moisturizer to give yourself a fresh look. Feeling good about your appearance can boost your overall confidence.

Build on Past Success: Your past achievements and successes are an indicator of future results. Remind yourself of challenges you've overcome. Use your positive track record as evidence of your capabilities. Create snippets, like a highlight reel, in your mind that exemplify some of your proudest accomplishments. By sharing these (see the previous section on storytelling) you are helping others understand the scope and complexity of your previous achievements, and this will also help boost your confidence.

Surround Yourself with Positivity: Engage with supportive and positive individuals. Surround yourself with people who are encouraging and uplifting, who believe in you and your Encore Career efforts. Of course, you can't always choose whom you engage with (i.e. family), but if you have someone in your life who is bringing you down, please try hard to limit your exposure to this negativity and criticism that may hinder your self-esteem. Intentionally seek out and spend time with the people who make you laugh, feel loved, and feel good about yourself. Hearing others speak positively about you enhances your positive self-perception, and this is a powerful confidence booster.

Track Your Progress: You may benefit from keeping a journal or documenting your milestone achievements, successes and positive experiences while establishing and growing your Encore Career. Reviewing your progress can reinforce a sense of achievement, and you can use it as a reminder of your capabilities during challenging times you may face. Your experience may even help inspire others in the future, so perhaps journal about your experiences with the intent to share them with others later.

Focus on Longer-Term Goals: Focusing on achievement of your goals and keeping your long-term vision in mind helps foster and maintain a growth mindset and a strong sense of purpose. These can be instrumental in countering negativity and boosting confidence.

Consistently applying these confidence-boosting strategies can contribute to a positive and confident mindset as you navigate your Encore Career. Remember that building self-confidence is a gradual process, and celebrating the small victories along the way is key to sustained growth.

Maintaining Resilience in the Face of Challenges

Resilience is the ability to adapt and bounce back from adversity. Resilience is valuable for staying flexible and open to change, and bouncing back stronger from setbacks, especially in the context of Encore Careers. Even if you are not feeling particularly resilient, it's okay. Building resilience is a skill that can be developed over time. Strategies for bolstering resilience may include things like reframing challenges, having a solution-focused approach, seeking support from family and friends, seeing challenges as opportunities to grow, and maintaining a positive mindset. Here are some strategies to bolster resilience in the face of challenges:

Reframing Challenges: Train yourself to look at the positive perspective of situations. View challenges as opportunities for growth and focus on achieving the potential positive outcomes rather than dwelling on difficulties or what may seem negative. Embrace a learning mindset by seeing challenges as chances to learn and develop new skills. Perceive and believe that each obstacle is a stepping stone to personal and professional improvement, practice self-reflection of learnings from your experiences.

Solution-Focused Approach: Identify solutions instead of getting overwhelmed by problems. Shift your focus to potential outcomes rather than what is getting in your way. Break down challenges into manageable parts and work on finding practical and achievable answers. By setting clear and realistic goals you will also be able to address specific aspects of the challenges in more manageable ways. Celebrate small wins as you make progress toward your objectives.

Seek Support: As we've said before, you don't need to go it alone. Build a support network for yourself. Cultivate relationships with family, friends, and mentors who can provide emotional support. Sharing your challenges and receiving empathy can alleviate stress. When needed, get professional guidance from colleagues, other professionals in your field, or a coach. Their insights and experiences can offer valuable perspectives.

Opportunities for Growth: Some people have developed a natural resiliency and can see the 'silver lining on every cloud'. If that is not you, don't worry. Resilience is a skill that can be developed. Embrace challenges as opportunities to enhance your resilience muscle and become more adept at navigating difficulties. Intentionally identify people who you notice practicing strong resilience, and gain an understanding of what they do that is different from your current approach. Try practicing some of their actions and see how it feels.

Maintaining a Positive Mindset: Cultivate optimism, because an optimistic outlook, even in challenging situations, can help build resilience. Believe in your ability to overcome difficulties and approach problems with a hopeful mindset. Practice gratitude. Express gratitude for the positive aspects of your life. This practice helps maintain a positive perspective and fosters resilience.

Self-Compassion: Be kind to yourself. Be compassionate toward yourself especially during tough times. Avoid self-criticism and recognize that everyone faces challenges. Learn from setbacks and give yourself positive reinforcement for taking risks, learning, and improving.

Mindfulness and Stress Reduction: Engage in mindfulness practices and techniques such as meditation or deep breathing exercises. These practices promote stress reduction and emotional regulation. Perhaps seek out a yin yoga class, or a meditation center. These are available in many locations as well as online. These techniques can be done without any equipment and when practiced for a few minutes a day can result in significantly reduced stress levels. You may also want to intentionally develop effective stress management strategies, such as understanding your stress triggers, to proactively prevent stressors from overwhelming you.

Healthy Lifestyle Habits: As with confidence building, physical well-being can also help strengthen resiliency. Prioritize your physical health through regular exercise, proper nutrition, and sufficient sleep. Strive for a healthy work-life balance, especially during your Encore Career, to prevent burnout. Allocate time for activities that bring joy and relaxation. Be conscientious about it - if you recognize that you were a 'workaholic' in your primary career, take intentional steps to avoid falling into this same practice in your third act.

Social Connection: Staying connected with your community and social groups has been shown to build resiliency, create a positive outlook on life, and some even attribute it to living longer. Participating in shared activities fosters a sense of belonging and support during challenging times, thereby reducing stress and building resilience.

Building resilience is an ongoing process that involves intentional effort and practice. By incorporating these strategies into your daily life, you can develop resilience as a foundational skill, enabling you to face challenges with greater strength and adaptability.

Prepare for a Double Whammy or Triple Whammy

So far, this chapter has addressed ways to deal with concerns about ageism and bias you may encounter when pursuing your Encore Career. If you are a woman you may need to be prepared for a double whammy. If you are a minority woman, you may be up against a triple whammy. In addition to ageism, women may also face gender-specific bias challenges and issues. As a minority, additional biases and stereotypes may also surface.

Some of the issues that women may need to deal with when navigating Encore Careers include:

Double Discrimination: Women may experience a form of double discrimination where ageism intersects with gender bias. They could face stereotypes and situations related to both their age and their gender. One example is lower earnings. Women have historically earned less than men, and this income gap can persist into your Encore Career. Being aware of this, it is important to know your worth, understand the market rates and pricing for your experience and services, and be willing to negotiate strongly for what you ought to get paid.

Balancing Caregiving Responsibilities: Many women continue to have caregiving responsibilities for children, grandchildren, spouses, parents, and other elderly family members. Balancing these responsibilities with an Encore Career can be challenging and may require additional support. As family dynamics change with age, women may find themselves being expected to take on caregiving roles, some may want to take on these responsibilities. This is okay as long as you keep in mind the impact that it will have on your availability for work and the pursuit of your Encore Career.

This transition requires careful planning and thought to ensure that everyone has their needs met while maintaining a sense of work-life balance where possible. Women, especially those with family responsibilities, may need to address work-life balance concerns more explicitly. This can involve setting boundaries, managing time effectively, asking for help, and enlisting others to help support you.

Access to Financing: If you are a woman considering entrepreneurship in your Encore Career, it is imperative that you know you may face unique challenges in securing financing. Women-owned businesses have historically received less investment and financing than those owned by men. Times are changing and there are more sources of investments, through loans, grants, and foundations, for women-owned businesses now than there were in the past. However, addressing the issues and challenges may require proactive planning, self-advocacy, and support from peers, mentors, and allies.

Certainly, just like women, minority individuals may face unique challenges and issues in their Encore Careers in the context of ageism and stereotypes. Some of the issues that minorities may need to address when navigating Encore Careers include:

Triple Discrimination: Ageism, with gender bias for women, and ethnic bias for minorities may end up as a triple whammy to overcome. This intersectionality compounds the effects of discrimination and bias. People in these situations need to have a strong sense of confidence and resilience along with a strong network to help them overcome potential challenges associated with launching their Encore Careers.

Inclusivity: Navigating Encore Careers is already challenging. Finding places with an active effort to build diversity, where individuals can actively advocate for equal representation and opportunities, where one's cultural identity and ethnic heritage are appreciated and respected can be a source of strength. Language and communication styles can be influenced by cultural backgrounds. Effective communication in the workplace may require addressing potential language barriers or variations in communication styles. Asking for help, self-advocacy, and raising awareness to get support from diversity and inclusion initiatives can help.

Navigating these challenges may require a combination of self-confidence, cultural pride, assertive advocacy, and the support of peers and allies. It's important to recognize that diversity and the unique perspectives that older workers, women, and minority individuals bring to the workforce are valuable assets and can contribute to a more inclusive and culturally rich work environment. Efforts to address these challenges can lead to greater equality and opportunities for people pursuing their Encore Careers.

In summary, this chapter is a call to action. By confidently showcasing your knowledge, wisdom, and expertise, you can defy age-related stereotypes, contribute significantly through your Encore Career, and potentially help shape a more inclusive workplace culture that treasures the collective strength of individuals from all age groups, genders, and ethnicities. Overcoming ageism, stereotypes, and biases is challenging. By understanding the challenges, employing strategies to combat the stereotypes and bias, and effectively demonstrating the value of your experience, you can navigate your Encore Career with confidence and resilience. This will help ensure you are recognized and valued for your contributions regardless of age, gender, and ethnicity.

CHAPTER 5
Who do you know that can help you? Networking and building connections.

"Nothing of significance was ever achieved by an individual acting alone. Look below the surface and you will find that all seemingly solo acts are really team efforts."
—John C. Maxwell

You may have noticed that the topic of networking has already been mentioned a few times in earlier chapters. This is because the power of networking can have a profound effect on your Encore Career. Effective networking is a key component of success in an Encore Career. Here we will dive deeper into how to leverage your network, build an online presence, and participate in professional organizations to nurture your Encore Career. This chapter equips you with the tools to expand your professional circle for the purpose of building and growing your Encore Career. Networking is an essential skill for those seeking to find opportunities, gain support, and share their expertise.

The Power of Networking

Networking is not just about collecting business cards or adding new LinkedIn connections. It is about building authentic, mutually beneficial, relationships. Networking is both a giving and receiving activity, and both are equally important. Networking enables you to both contribute to the success of others and seek support and opportunities for yourself. We do this by building genuine relationships, showing a sincere interest in others, and being generous with our time and resources.

Some people enjoy networking while others would rather have a root canal. Interestingly, neuroscience studies show that networking can bring you joy and positivity! Engaging in positive social interactions, such as networking, increases a feeling of personal well-being. Behaving altruistically or with empathy triggers the release of oxytocin - the hormone associated with human bonding - and this makes you feel good. And another good reason to network is that seeking and sharing advice, new perspectives and information will help you learn new things.

Building and Leveraging a Strong Network

Building a strong network is not a one-time endeavor; it's an ongoing process. There are many reasons (a.k.a. excuses) why people may choose not to network. Some of the reasons are: concerns you won't be good at it, it takes time away from other priorities, concerns about people not wanting to get to know you, you just don't want to become involved in anything new, people will think you are too old, concerns that you don't have anything to offer, or maybe you are just a shy person.

By putting these reasons to not do it aside and focusing on the positives of networking, you will be able to leverage your network while continuing to build your networking skills and relationships. Here are some strategies for effective networking:

<u>Be authentic:</u> Authenticity is at the core of networking success. Determine what your goals are for networking and be purposeful in your actions. Building a diverse network will be beneficial, as we've mentioned before. When networking, keep in mind that what you say, who you say it to, how you say it, and why you say it are all important. Being consistent with your professional brand (see previous chapter) and how you want to be perceived by others is part of networking.

<u>Be curious:</u> Listen and be willing to hear what others are saying. Practice active listening, which involves genuinely engaging in conversations and showing interest in the ideas and needs of others. Try to avoid listening just to respond or to reply in a superficial way. This is not an authentic way of interacting with others. Be fully present in the conversation and appreciative of their time and sharing of information. Perhaps share articles or books related to your common interests, ask if they have any recommendations as well.

<u>Be vulnerable:</u> Admit you don't have all the answers, seek to learn. Being vulnerable means letting others see the sides of you about which you have less confidence or certainty. Allow others that you trust to

help you, but steer clear of people who are just trying to take advantage of you.

Assess your current connections: Without even trying, you have a network of people who know you, professionally and personally. Over the years of school, multiple jobs, career shifts, changes in where you live and socialize, have created valuable network connections. Whether it's former colleagues, friends, or industry contacts, these connections can provide support, leads about job opportunities, and guidance for pursuing your Encore Career. Even people who know you through family relationships, people in your neighborhood, or at your yoga class, even people you met years ago at your kid's school, etc. Sometimes your personal and professional lives collide.

Assess your current network connections to see who can support you in building your Encore Career. Be sure that your network is not just people similar to you. Differences in experience, expertise, background, gender, ethnicity, age, etc. add so much value to your network. You can expect that your network connections will also have different levels of influence, and some are closer to you while others are more distant. Here are some questions to start thinking about:

Do you have or need mentors? This is someone who guides you by building trust and modeling positive behaviors. An effective mentor understands that their role is to be dependable, engaged, authentic, and tuned into your needs. Having both formal and informal mentors is ideal for your network. A mentor may share information about his or her own career path, as well as provide guidance, motivation, emotional support, and role modeling. A mentor may help you with exploring Encore Careers, setting goals, developing contacts, and identifying resources.

Do you have or need sponsors? This is someone in a position of power who uses their influence to advocate on your behalf and who knows you well enough to put his or her reputation on the line for you. This person can offer greater visibility, make meaningful business connections for you, and offer advice.

Do you have or need advocates? These are people who publicly support and recommend you. They trust that you will deliver, they always have your best interest at heart, and usually expect nothing in return.

Do *you have or need allies*? While they might appear as friends or advocates, their loyalty is more conditional. They will endorse you, but only as long as it also serves their own purpose. This gives the appearance of being a trusted confidant, however, conditional relationships change based upon the circumstances. Be aware that their level of commitment to your success is likely to waiver, especially when conditions change.

Do you have an *Encourager* (someone you can lean on when you are feeling down), a *Challenger* (someone who asks the tough questions and makes you think about whether you are using the best approach), and a *Technical Advisor* (someone who is always up on the latest trends and perspectives and willing to share this information). Think of these three roles as your Encore Career 'board of directors'.

<u>Target new connections with purpose:</u> Who are individuals and groups who can provide the most valuable support and opportunities to you? Strive for diversity of age, ethnicity, and purpose. Some people will help you generate leads for your new business, others will help with technical advice, or offer empathy or encouragement when needed. Others will serve as role models representing what you aspire to become. Understand that you can add value and help others too. Seek out people for your network who could benefit from what you are offering.

<u>Networking Opportunities:</u> Navigating various networking events, both in-person and online, and making the most of them can be challenging but not impossible. When attending networking events, remember *it is more important to be interested than interesting*. Be prepared with some typical questions and listen to the answers. Also, be prepared to answer these questions for yourself, such as:

- *Tell me about yourself, what business are you in?*
- *How long have you been doing that?*
- *What are your professional goals? What are you striving to achieve?*
- *What are trends in your industry? Where do you see opportunities to capitalize on these trends?*

Leveraging Social Media: Utilizing social media platforms for networking purposes and for building business leads has become the norm. There are many platforms ranging from the well-known LinkedIn, Facebook, TikTok, Instagram, Pinterest, and Snapchat, to lesser-known ones and others that have private social networking groups requiring sponsorship and sometimes paid memberships. You can do an internet search on all the different platforms to see which ones are right for you. If you are not familiar or comfortable with using social media to build your network, that might be okay, depending on who your target audience is. As we are in a digital age, it is important to have a presence in as many areas as you can on social media. For many, outsourcing your social media content creation will both save you time and further establish yourself as an authoritative figure in your field. In the next chapter, we are going to further discuss the value of building an online presence.

Giving Back Through Networking: Contributing to the success of others is a key component of networking. Offer support to others in your network when the opportunity arises. Mentorship is a powerful form of networking, and typically benefits both the mentor and the mentee. Many professional organizations have formal mentoring programs you can participate in. You may uncover other volunteer opportunities through your professional networking such as becoming an advisor or taking on a volunteer leadership role in your professional networking organization.

Reconnecting and Rekindling Relationships: Reconnecting with past contacts and nurturing existing relationships through periodic communication enables you to keep up with each other's lives and careers. Staying in touch is easy through LinkedIn messages, texts, or through emails, especially if you are not living close to each other. Video calls, phone calls, or in person meetings periodically can be arranged, too.

Seeking Guidance: Being open to seeking guidance and advice from those with relevant expertise is a great way to leverage your network. Getting clear on your goals and communicating clearly about your Encore Career aspirations with your network may gain you supporters, reveal some new ideas, and provide you with things you've not thought of before.

Informational Interviews: Informational interviews allow you to learn more about things, without the purpose of seeking help. Engage in informational interviews with experienced contacts to gain insights and learn about potential opportunities. In addition, your network may be able to make introductions for you to people with whom you might not have access to otherwise, and to engage in additional informational interviews.

Industry Insights: Once you are out on your own, pursuing your Encore Career, you may no longer have access to certain information about your industry. It could be advantageous to tap into the industry expertise and access of your network connections to stay informed about current trends and developments.

Express gratitude: Remember to demonstrate your appreciation and gratitude for the assistance, advice, and new connections that have been provided by your network connections. No one appreciates being taken advantage of, so be sure you are not over-expecting from certain people in your network and you are practicing reciprocity.

Resilience: Networking is not only a tool for career advancement but also a source of resilience. Your network can provide a support system during challenges, offer insights into overcoming obstacles, and create a sense of belonging and community during your Encore Career journey.

Building an Online Presence: Do you need one?

In today's contemporary digital age, an online presence could be crucial for professional success. You can do as little as creating a professional LinkedIn profile, or further strengthen your online presence with a website and social media accounts. Depending on what you choose for your Encore Career, who your target audience is, and what work you are pursuing, there are ways to effectively showcase your skills, experience, and interests using different avenues.

Maximizing Digital Platforms for Encore Career Success

Creating and maintaining a strong online footprint can be a game-changer for your Encore Career. Having an online presence is more than just a digital resume; it's a means to communicate your professional brand, exploit your expertise, and share your professional identity to a broader audience.

Start with a Professional LinkedIn Profile

LinkedIn is a cornerstone of professional networking and online visibility. Every professional ought to have a LinkedIn profile and can be using it to build their professional network. To optimize your LinkedIn profile and maximize the visibility of your LinkedIn profile:

- Be sure to include a catchy headline using relevant keywords, have a professional profile picture, and customize the top border of your profile to reflect your career/interests/passions.
- Indicate that you are open to work and/or providing services, using the functionality of LinkedIn. This will automatically, through the magic of algorithms, gain you greater visibility to people who are doing searches on LinkedIn for professionals with your experience.
- Use your About section to tell people what you are doing, highlight past achievements, and showcase your skills. This can also be a version of your UVP as mentioned in the previous chapter.
- Summarize your work experiences with relevant information that supports your Encore Career. Remove unnecessary or irrelevant information.
- Gain recommendations and endorsements to stand out among your connections.
- Select up to 50 skills that you want to spotlight, ensuring that the majority of them are relevant to what you want to do next, in your Encore Career.
- Use the LinkedIn recommendations or search bar to connect with colleagues, industry peers, experts, and mentors to expand your network and reach.

- Engage with LinkedIn professional groups that align with your interests and Encore Career goals. This can gain you greater exposure to new ideas through their posts, and if you want to share your expertise you can post on their group site as well.

Developing a Personal Website

A personal website can serve as a central hub for your online presence. The process of developing a personal website can be daunting. If you feel this is the case, you can hire someone to create the website for you. Consider what is involved:

- Selecting a Domain Name: Choosing a domain name that reflects your professional identity.
- Creating a Portfolio: Showcasing your work, achievements, and expertise through an online portfolio.
- Contact Information: Ensuring that your contact information is readily available for potential employers or collaborators.
- Blogging and Content Sharing: The value of regularly sharing your insights, knowledge, and passions through a blog or other content-sharing platforms.
- Accepting payments: Some sites are commerce-enabled so you can accept payments directly through your website if this is something that makes sense for you.

Leveraging Social Media Platforms

Social media platforms extend your digital reach and enable you to connect with a broader audience. There are certain considerations for how to effectively use social media platforms for professional purposes, including:

- Choosing the Right Platforms: identifying which social media platforms are most relevant to your Encore Career goals.
- Professional Engagement: maintaining a professional tone and engaging with industry-related discussions.
- Building a Thought Leadership Presence: showcasing your expertise and becoming a thought leader in your chosen field.

- Creating and Managing a Content Strategy that aligns with your Encore Career goals: to ensure content consistency and frequency of content posting, it may be important for you to consider your online presence. Creating a content calendar and managing your digital content effectively may be a strategy that is important for you.

The Significance of Content Strategy: Content is the vehicle through which you communicate your professional identity and expertise. A well-crafted content strategy helps ensure that your content aligns with your Encore Career aspirations and reaches the right audience. Your content may include thought leadership, industry insights, or sharing personal achievements and inspirational stories. Creating themes for your content will help you to maintain relevance and develop a rapport with your target audiences. You may decide that you need some help with a content strategy and content management. There are many people who offer this type of support as a service.

Creating a Content Calendar: Crafting a content calendar can help with consistency and frequency of your content sharing. You would start by setting publication dates. Perhaps you choose to regularly post two times per week. What days would be best? For which publications will you post?

Audience Engagement: Incorporating content that engages with your audience, such as Q&A sessions, polls, or challenges can help generate interest in your posts. For example, on LinkedIn, when one of your connections engages with your content post, their network is notified, and your content is then suggested to those additional people. They could become potential new connections for you - this is how you can extend your reach in an ongoing manner without much effort.

Managing Digital Content: Effectively managing your digital content is essential to maintaining a strong online presence. Producing content that aligns with your content strategy and Encore Career objectives, editing and proofreading your posts to ensure that your content is error-free and of high quality, using visuals such as images and infographics will enhance the appeal of your content.

A more advanced digital content strategy may include things such as search engine optimization (SEO) which helps to increase the discoverability of your content, ongoing monitoring and tracking of how well your audience responds to your content and making adjustments accordingly, and measuring the impact and reach of your content through analytics and key performance indicators (KPIs).

Evolving Your Content Strategy: Over time you may want to evolve your content strategy based on audience feedback, changing industry trends, and your own Encore Career growth.

A well-structured content strategy, aligned with your Encore Career goals, enables you to effectively communicate your professional identity, demonstrate your expertise, and potentially build business leads to help grow your Encore Career business and opportunities.

If You Are Active Online, You May Need to Safeguard Your Digital Brand

In today's digital age, the internet serves as a repository of information about individuals, and your online reputation has a significant influence on your professional opportunities and personal life. Online reputation management could be a vital aspect of building your online presence. Here we offer some strategies for monitoring and maintaining a positive online reputation, as well as addressing any issues or negative feedback professionally.

Monitoring Your Online Reputation: Be aware of what is being said about you on the internet. You can do this by setting up Google alerts to receive notifications when your name or keywords associated with you are mentioned online. A more advanced digital strategy may include employing social media listening tools to monitor discussions and mentions on your different social platforms. Alternatively, hiring a reputation management service will provide you with a comprehensive monitoring and analysis of your online presence.

Maintaining a Positive Online Reputation: Cultivating a positive online reputation can build trust with potential employers, collaborators, and clients, and contribute to your Encore Career success. Be sure to employ a discipline of professionalism in your tone and demeanor for all online interactions, ensure the quality of your content reflects your professional expertise and the brand reputation you are intending, engage with your audience in a constructive and respectful manner, and be transparent and truthful in your online activities especially when giving your opinion. Be conscientious of the impact of your content - especially if what you post might engage one group but potentially offend another.

Addressing Negative Feedback: Even with the best efforts, negative feedback or unfavorable reactions to your content may arise. First assess the validity of the negative feedback and decide whether it warrants a response. If you will respond, be sure to craft a constructive, professional response. Perhaps have a trusted advisor review it before you post your response to ensure you are not taking an emotional or defensive stance. It might be best to respond to the negative feedback privately rather than post a reply. If the negative feedback is particularly defamatory, damaging to your reputation, and could impact your credibility, you may want to seek legal advice.

Know How To Set Your Online Privacy and Security Settings: Social media platforms understand the importance of online privacy and security. Most of them will offer settings that help you to protect your personal information and online presence from potential threats, including identity theft and cyberattacks. If you find yourself in the unfortunate circumstance of facing particularly challenging online reputation issues or a security breach, we suggest you seek professional assistance, such as reputation management firms or legal counsel, to address and resolve complex situations.

Networking Through Professional Organizations

Joining professional organizations can be a valuable step towards building new connections and strengthening existing ones. There are many reasons that joining a professional organization can bring value. These organizations typically offer a relevant, structured, and purposeful environment for making new networking connections, keeping up with industry trends, learning new skills, and attending professional development events. Some organizations have membership fees and fees to attend their events. These are usually nominal relative to the value you will receive from them if you take full advantage of your memberships.

It is important to identify and select the applicable organizations to support your Encore Career. Choose groups who align with your Encore Career goals and interests, as well as explore others that may introduce you to new ways of approaching things. Here we provide some guidance on how to identify and select the right organizations, how to actively participate in their activities, and how to network effectively within these groups.

Do Your Research: Conduct research to identify professional organizations relevant to your field or industry. Determine if having a local chapter is important to you, or if a virtual membership suits your needs. It is usually easy to find the websites for professional organizations through an internet search. Review the group's online presence, see who their members are, who are their sponsoring organizations. Evaluate their structure and offerings to see if they are a fit for what you are looking for.

Assess Membership Benefits: Evaluate the benefits and resources offered by different organizations. Some may have different levels of membership at different costs. Some may offer both local, national, and virtual membership options. Determine what value the organizations will provide to you for things such as expanding your networking opportunities, learning and development, and if you want to share your expertise, you might explore being a speaker or presenter for the group.

Actively Participating in Organization Activities: To reap the greatest benefits of membership, it is important to dedicate the time to actively participate. Whether there is a local chapter or a virtual chapter, it is important to commit to attending a few events each year - these may be networking events, seminars, webinars, and conferences. Joining committees or subgroups within the organization is a great way to contribute as well as build deeper connections with other members.

Taking on a volunteer leadership position in a professional organization can bring even more visibility to your online presence and professional brand (you would certainly want to include this role on your LinkedIn profile.) Offering your expertise or insights through presentations, workshops, or sharing articles with other members can also deepen your relationships.

You may want to consider memberships in multiple professional organizations. Keep in mind that each will take time to attend events and foster relationships to gain the most value from them. This could be an effective strategy for you as long as each one provides you with specific value, and you feel you will be able to balance and leverage these memberships effectively.

Effective Networking With Professional Organizations

Networking within professional organizations is typically a central focus of the members. Most members are eager to make new connections and build their professional brand through the organization's membership. Prioritize building genuine and authentic relationships with fellow members. Practice active listening during conversations to learn about the needs and goals of others and try to help them in their own journey. Be willing to offer assistance or resources to others within the organization as this will help build your reputation and brand. Maintaining a consistent presence within the organization by attending events and participating in discussions will help you become recognizable.

Leveraging your memberships in professional organizations can also set you up for Encore Career success. Membership in these organizations can open doors to new opportunities, provide you with job leads you may not have otherwise known about, set you up for potential collaborations on complex projects, and offer the opportunity to be a mentor or to be mentored by other members. Many professional organizations offer resources such as white papers, online courses, and help members to gain certifications that can enhance your skills, knowledge, branding, and credibility in your field.

Industry events and conferences sponsored by professional organizations are ideal places for networking, learning, and staying updated on industry trends. These events, whether in-person or conducted virtually, can be great experiences and are excellent for building your network with connections in your field. Attending events can be costly, so be sure to find those that align with your specific Encore Career goals and interests. Research the event location, the planned agenda, the costs, who the speakers will be, and who the attendees will be.

Maximize your event participation by actively participating in sessions, workshops, or panel discussions. While you might be there to gain knowledge, you may also have knowledge that other attendees may find valuable. During breaks, don't be afraid to approach new people, introduce yourself (great opportunity to use your UVP) and initiate conversations to build connections. Remember, as we said earlier, it is more important to be interested than interesting, so be sure to ask thoughtful questions when you are meeting new people, and also ask engaging questions during Q&A sessions or discussions.

Many events now use Apps to provide attendees with the agenda, announcements, and updates during the events, and they will usually also provide a list of the attendees and speakers - so this is another way you can build your network by connecting with them during the event or follow up afterwards.

Effective networking extends beyond initial introductions. Be sure to take the time to follow-up with people you've met, connect with them on LinkedIn as well, and nurture the connections by sharing insights and providing value to your network connections over time. Focusing on the quality and longevity of relationships is something to continue throughout your Encore Career.

In summary, Chapter 5 has illuminated the transformative power of networking in an Encore Career. We've underscored the significance of building mutually beneficial relationships, that networking is a two-way street, and with the right skills, mindset, and commitment, networking can open doors, provide guidance, and foster professional growth and success in your third act. Creating an online presence may be a very important component of your Encore Career networking and brand strategy, or maybe not, depending on who your target audience is. Memberships in professional organizations and attending industry events and conferences can have a profoundly positive impact on your Encore Career for networking, learning, and staying updated on industry trends. By actively participating, initiating conversations, and following up with new contacts, you can harness the full potential of networking to advance your Encore Career goals.

CHAPTER 6

Preparing your finances as you transition to your Encore Career.

"What would you do if you weren't afraid?"
—Sheryl Sandberg

Considering the financial aspects of transitioning into an Encore Career are important. In this chapter we will address budgeting, financial planning, managing healthcare and insurance, and saving for retirement. This chapter only intends to provide a foundational knowledge and address common financial concerns. We strongly encourage you to speak with a professional Financial Advisor to ensure that you have the appropriate information for your personal situation. There are financial advisors who specialize in supporting people who are moving towards retirement, and they can provide you with personalized guidance and expertise.

Things you need to know about post-retirement income

Check with your financial advisor to understand any limitations on your finances and ability to earn in a post-retirement career. Government treatment of income will vary depending on what country you are in and how much time you spend there. It may also vary domestically as some U.S. states have no income tax. Some other considerations may be dependent on how old you are, your spouse's age if you are married, your eligibility for government program income, timing of/age at which you begin taking payments, as well as additional sources of income you may have. Laws and regulations vary greatly and can change, so be sure to choose a qualified Financial Advisor who is able to guide you in your journey and decision-making based on your unique circumstances.

Aligning Financial Resources with Lifestyle and Encore Career Goals

Considering the aspects of financial planning and preparation as you move towards your Encore Career, and depending on what you choose to do in your third act, you may be able to make certain assumptions. For example, will you work fewer hours or reduce the earning level of your annual income? This will need to be considered in alignment with your evolving lifestyle. Will you choose to 'downsize' or move to a different location during this time? This may reduce or increase your expenses longer-term. What type of activities do you want to enjoy and what costs do you need to budget to support these? All these types of changes should be viewed as considerations during this transition period from primary career to Encore Career.

- Assessing Lifestyle Needs: evaluating the financial requirements of the desired Encore Career and post-retirement lifestyle.
- Creating a Financial Plan: developing a comprehensive financial plan that encompasses income sources, expenses, savings, investments, and contingencies.
- Setting and Revisiting Financial Goals: periodically revisiting financial goals as career or personal circumstances change.
- Balancing Short-Term and Long-Term Goals: finding a balance between immediate financial needs and long-term financial security.

Financial Security and Peace of Mind

Having a full view of your financial situation can provide a sense of financial security and can bring peace of mind. According to Tiffany Keefe, a certified Financial Advisor and Wealth Manager in Georgia, USA, "Probably the most common question we get asked is, '*How can I make sure I won't run out of money in retirement?*' Everyone has a magic number or dollar amount they would like saved. This dollar amount is a number that would put their mind at ease and help them sleep through the night. Our goal is to help them better understand what that amount is and co-create a plan on how to get them there." Other questions that are frequently asked when meeting with a Financial Advisor, and may also be on your mind, include:

Am I on the right track with my investments?
Are my investments in the right places?
Am I receiving the right value for my investment fees?
Are there ways I could be saving on taxes, or create tax-free income after I retire?
What kind of planning do I need to do to avoid becoming a financial burden to my family?

Effective financial preparation can also help to reduce some of the stress or anxiety that may naturally occur during the transition from primary career to Encore Career. A well-thought-out financial plan can also empower you to make important career and lifestyle choices with confidence. A professional Financial Advisor can help you sort out and make sense of your retirement investments, such as employer-sponsored retirement plans (401ks, pensions) and individual retirement accounts (IRAs) and their tax implications, as well as guide you towards moderate or lower risk investment vehicles that can help in securing financial stability for your Encore Career and beyond.

Having full visibility to your financial situation and an effective financial plan can also influence the choices you make in your Encore Career. A strong financial foundation can provide the freedom to explore new opportunities, start a business, or engage in volunteer work without being solely driven by financial necessity, while balancing that with a lifestyle of your choosing.

Understanding the Multifaceted Nature of Financial Preparation

Financial preparation and planning for your later years typically begins much earlier in your career. As you consider your Encore Career, financial planning is not solely about the amount of money you have saved or will be earning. It is about holistically aligning your financial resources with your evolving lifestyle and encore career goals. Financial preparation is not a one-dimensional concept but is multifaceted, by that we mean it can encompass various elements such as:

<u>Budgeting:</u> creating a budget that accounts for known expenses, income, savings; having emergency funds established or setting aside funds for unexpected expenses or setbacks.

Insurance and Healthcare expenses: evaluating and obtaining appropriate insurance coverage to mitigate financial risks.

Longer-term Financial Planning: planning for both the Encore Career and traditional full retirement; investment decisions to grow and safeguard your financial assets; and estate planning for the longer-term disposition of assets and wealth.

Next, we will dive a bit deeper into each of these elements.

Budgeting

If you have not been a budgeter before, you may find the activity of creating a budget a bit daunting. However, we encourage you to consider at least starting with outlining an estimated budget that reflects your Encore Career aspirations. This could include estimating expenses based on your assumptions, and including any additional costs associated with the transitions you will be making associated with your Encore Career and desired lifestyle.

A simple budget may start with estimates for:

- Living Expenses: this encompasses basic costs such as housing, utilities, groceries, insurance, and transportation. A best practice is also to have three to six months of living expenses saved as an emergency fund.
- Lifestyle Expenses: this would include hobbies, sports, and their associated costs.
- Travel Expenses: considering potential travel expenses, whether for work-related trips or personal enrichment.
- Workspace and Equipment: planning for a dedicated workspace or any equipment required for your Encore Career.
- Education or Reskilling Costs: identifying expenses related to acquiring new skills, certifications, or education related to your Encore Career plans.

You can establish this initial budget on a simple spreadsheet, and it is enough to get started in conversations with your Financial Advisor.

If you are an experienced budgeter, you may prefer to use a more comprehensive budgeting tool or app that is designed to help you manage your budget. There are many to choose from, but keep in mind that some budgeting tools and apps have annual costs, different security features, and various account integration capabilities. Check their ratings and reviews before deciding on what to use.

A more comprehensive budget process may include:

- Tracking Current Expenses: reviewing current expenses to understand spending patterns and assuming any changes that will occur due to decisions you are making.
- Identifying Income Sources: identifying all sources of income including pensions, retirement savings accounts, general savings, potential government income, part-time work, investment returns, or any other sources of income.
- Setting Financial Goals: determining financial goals that align with your Encore Career vision and aligning the future budget with these goals.
- Allocating Resources: Allocating resources to different expense categories, ensuring that there's a clear financial plan and visibility of what money comes in and what goes out.
- Researching reskilling and education costs: estimating the costs of courses, workshops, certifications, or degrees, as well as identifying potential sources of financial aid or scholarships.

Adjusting the Budget as Needed

Budgeting for your Encore Career and lifestyle expenses doesn't have to be overwhelming, and there are online budgeting tools and calculators that can help you. It is also important to note that budgeting is like a forecast. It can change and should not be static, budget management is an ongoing process. It is important to regularly assess your budget and make adjustments as your Encore Career plans progress and evolve and other aspects of your life continue to change.

Insurance and Healthcare Expenses

Healthcare can be a major financial consideration and can be complex, depending on where you live, if you will receive retirement benefits from an employer, your eligibility for expenses to be supplemented, and other considerations. Each country has a different approach to healthcare and whether it is legally required, government funded, etc.

In general, if you live in a country that provides universal health coverage, then your financial risk is quite low. If you live in a country, like the US, where individuals pay for their own healthcare, then your financial risk is significantly greater. However, states across the US also differ in their coverage. Therefore, as you transition into your Encore Career, we encourage you to be aware of the different particulars for your healthcare and insurance plan options as these can vary based on where you live, your health, and your personal financial situation.

This book could not possibly highlight all the potential differences you may need to know, so for the purpose of this section we will provide general insights into the financial implications of health care expense management to be considered when transitioning into your Encore Career. You can find more specific reliable resources for additional information about insurance options and healthcare coverage on the internet.

Managing Healthcare Expenses

When considering, estimating, and managing healthcare expenses, keep these in mind:

- Compare Health Insurance Plans: evaluate and select the health insurance plans that align with your healthcare needs and for any others whom you continue to cover under your health plan. Costs and coverages vary greatly. Depending on income levels, there are government subsidized plans as well. Some countries legally require all residents to have a minimum level of coverage.
- Budget for Healthcare: incorporate healthcare costs into your overall budget, accounting for premiums, deductibles, copayments, and estimated out-of-pocket expenses depending on the plan you select.
- Maximize Health Care Savings (i.e. Health Savings Accounts (HSAs) in the US): understand and maximize the benefits of contributing to an HSA for the greatest tax-advantaged healthcare savings. You can use HSA funds to pay for deductibles, copayments, coinsurance, and other qualified medical

expenses such as prescriptions and some health-related over-the-counter purchases. Withdrawals to pay eligible medical expenses are tax-free and unspent HSA funds roll over from year to year, allowing you to build tax-free savings to pay for medical care later.

- Long-Term Care Expense Planning: this type of healthcare includes a range of services and supports daily living, such as assistance with activities like bathing, dressing, and meal preparation. Depending on how you intend to be cared for long-term, these types of care expenses should be considered in your overall financial plan. Long-Term Care Insurance plans and costs vary, and options should be researched before deciding.

Understanding Medicare (for US residents)

Medicare is the US federal health insurance program for individuals aged 65 and older and those with certain disabilities. There are multiple Medicare Parts including: Part A (hospital insurance), Part B (medical insurance), Part C (Medicare Advantage), and Part D (prescription drug coverage). It is important for you to know and understand your Medicare enrollment and eligibility time frame and the process for enrolling, because if you miss the initial enrollment opportunity this could be problematic later on. In addition to Medicare, many people choose to supplement their coverage with supplemental insurance such as Medigap policies, because traditional Medicare may not fully provide all the coverage you need.

Estimating and making assumptions about your potential healthcare needs and costs as you transition into your Encore Career can be complicated. Consider your health status and potential healthcare expenses as part of your retirement planning and revisit your forecasts and estimates periodically as things can change.

Longer-term Financial Planning and Retirement Considerations

As we discussed earlier, a budget allows you to see what expenses you will have and the income you will need to cover those expenses.

Financial planning encompasses aspects such as multiple income streams, investments, and retirement accounts. Financial planning involves a holistic approach, taking into account both immediate financial needs and longer-term financial security.

Terminology to be familiar with as you converse with your Financial Advisors may include:

- Multiple Sources of Income: exploring various sources of income, such as part-time work, investments, pensions, and Encore Career earnings.
- Creating Passive Income: strategies for generating passive income through investments, real estate, or intellectual property.
- Retirement Accounts: understand the different types of retirement accounts, including employer-sponsored retirement plans, IRAs, and annuities.
- Risk Assessment: analysis determining how much risk and potential costs for the risk that exist in your portfolio.
- Rollovers and Transfers: the process of rolling over or transferring retirement funds from different investment vehicles to better align with your Encore Career transition and income needs.
- Investment Strategies: asset allocation, risk management, and tax-efficient investing to optimize returns and minimize tax burdens.
- Social Security and Timing (for US residents): estimated Social Security benefits, the importance of timing when it comes to drawing Social Security benefits, understanding eligibility requirements, how Social Security benefits are calculated, determining the optimal time to start receiving Social Security benefits to maximize payouts, and how Social Security decisions can align with Encore Career plans.
- Estate Planning: Preparing for the disposition of assets and wealth, including wills, trusts, and beneficiaries.

According to Tiffany Keefe, "a professional Financial Advisor can help determine the strengths and weaknesses of a plan and offer solutions that best fit the client's goals. We can also run through different scenarios, or what if's, to make sure your financial plan is sound and designed to handle unexpected changes."

In summary, we looked at financial preparation, planning, and retirement considerations in the context of your Encore Career. The considerations of importance include having full visibility to your expenses and income streams, budgeting and managing for planned and unexpected expenses, healthcare costs, and becoming familiar with terminology related to creating financial security and peace of mind as you work towards your Encore Career vision. We also want to reiterate the importance of getting a professional Financial Advisor to help you through this financial preparation and planning process.

CHAPTER 7
What do I need to learn?

"Don't be intimidated by what you don't know. That can be your greatest strength and ensure that you do things differently from everyone else." **—Sara Blakely**

As mentioned in earlier chapters, lifelong learning is a vital component for success in an Encore Career. Being a lifelong learner includes nurturing an open and curious mindset, being able to see things from multiple angles, and often results in new ways of approaching life. Lifelong learning may involve acquiring new skills and knowledge through formal or informal learning environments, perhaps advancing or recertifying your professional credentials. There are many options for continuing to learn - books, magazines, websites, in person classes, online courses, mentors, social media channels, and podcasts. Balancing learning with your Encore Career work and personal life should be a key focus.

The world is constantly evolving, and staying up to date with industry trends and emerging technologies is essential for Encore Career sustainability. In Chapter 3, we provided a long list of resources for lifelong learning in general. In this chapter we will focus on purposeful learning as it relates specifically to your Encore Career.

Identifying Relevant Skills and Knowledge Gaps

You may need to put your ego aside if you've already been an expert in your field during your earlier career. As you reflect on your skills and knowledge, you will need to be able to admit that there may be areas in which you could benefit from upskilling or reskilling as they pertain to your Encore Career. Upskilling is to expand knowledge, skills, and competencies that you already have, while reskilling is to learn completely new skills and acquire new knowledge and competency in an unfamiliar area.

The steps to take for upskilling are:

1. assess what you know today
2. determine what you need to know for your Encore Career
3. identify ways to close the gap between the two

The process to take for reskilling is to:

1. determine what you need to know for your Encore Career
2. assess what you know today relative to #1
3. identify ways to close the gap between the two

While it may seem subtle, the difference is where you begin your assessment. This process of introspection should help you target specific areas for development or improvement depending on whether your Encore Career plan is building on what you already know or is taking you into a brand new direction.

Reflect on Current Skills and Competencies, Identify Gaps

If you know what you want your Encore Career path to be, then reflecting on your current competencies and skills, as they relate to the role you will hold, is the first step of this introspective process.

- Conduct a skills inventory: create a list of your current skills and the competencies you developed over a lifetime of experiences. Here are a couple hints: you may want to put the list into a spreadsheet that you can use to order/reorder and filter on later. You may also want to use a resource list of skills and competencies for different types of roles - these can be found by searching the internet - because you may not realize just how many skills and competencies you have. Select up to 50 skills and competencies for this exercise; remember to list use of certain technology and tools as well.
- Rank Them: once you've put your skills and competencies into the spreadsheet, then rank order them as they relate to your strengths, for example on a scale of 1 to 3, assign a 1 to your top skills and 2 or 3 to your weaker skills. This will help you identify areas of strength as well as potential weaknesses

that may need to be addressed as they relate to your choice of Encore Careers.

- Next, compile a list of the skills and competencies needed for your desired Encore Career role, order them in rank order of importance or impact. You may want to use job descriptions found online to gather this information, along with the skills list you collected earlier.
- Compare your existing skills and level of strength to the skills required in the desired Encore Career path. Note any gaps in skills and any areas that could be improved and focus on the top 10 skills to begin with. They will likely have the greatest impact on your success.
- Seek External Feedback and Validation: by seeking input from others who know you well enough and will give you honest answers - such as mentors, career advisors, or peers - you can gain an external perspective on the skills and knowledge gaps you've identified.
- Industry Trends: Catching up and staying updated on the latest industry trends and evolving skill requirements in your chosen field could be important, depending on how quickly things like the technology, tools, and priorities of that industry might shift.

Creating Your Development Plan

Once you've gone through the process of identifying the top skills and competencies to either upskill or reskill, it's time to create your development plan. Based on the skills and knowledge gaps identified, you will want to next identify your options for the targeted growth areas. Key steps include:

- Set Clear Objectives: define clear objectives for your skill and competency development, including what skills and knowledge is needed, why it is important to acquire them, and a timeline for achieving proficiency. Your prioritization may be dependent on urgency and impact.
- Determine How You Learn Best: you may want to consider "how" you learn best - visual (use videos, create diagrams), auditory (use podcasts, audio from video, mentors, attend discussion groups), reading/writing (take notes, download

transcripts), or hands-on (attend labs, in person learning settings).

- Consider Investments: at this stage in your life, how much time, effort, and cost do you want to invest into formal or informal learning methods. How much do the credentials matter vs. actual experience? Would a micro-certification add to your credibility?
- Choose a Learning Method: by identifying the most suitable learning methods for each skill or competency, you will be providing yourself with options. You may find that one source, such as a formal learning course, can help you develop multiple skills. Perhaps a workshop will be focused on one particular skill or competency. If you are self-motivated you may set yourself some goals to complete a self-study, or if appropriate you may find a mentor.
- Technology and Tools: Exploring available resources either online or in your community, you may find specific training, tutorials, job aids, and tools for acquiring the necessary knowledge and skills.

Exploring Formal Educational Options

A wide array of educational opportunities is available to individuals seeking to acquire new skills or knowledge. Various options include traditional degree programs, online courses, certifications, micro-certifications, workshops, and bootcamps. There are advantages and disadvantages of each option, so we hope to enable you to make an informed decision about which avenue aligns best with your goals.

Traditional Degree Programs

<u>In-Depth Learning:</u> the depth of knowledge provided by degree programs is often significant, offering a comprehensive understanding of specific subjects.

<u>Time Commitment:</u> the time commitment required for completing a traditional degree, usually two to four years depending on the degree program, must be considered for balancing along with other responsibilities. Some degree programs are only offered in person on

campus, other degree programs are offered in an online setting, and others offer a hybrid schedule.

Cost: traditional degree program tuition can run from $6,000 to upwards of $50,000 per year depending on the school, duration of the program, and level of the degree.

Online Courses and E-Learning

Flexibility and Convenience: the flexibility of online courses allows learners to study at their own convenience. Most online courses have a curriculum that encourages learners to keep a certain pace of study and to see it through to completion. Most online courses do not require prerequisites, and many have multiple levels of learning ranging from basic, to intermediate, to advanced depending on your learning needs.

Diverse Course Offerings: the wide variety of subjects available online may be appealing depending on your diverse interests and development needs. Websites such as Udemy.com, Coursera.com, LinkedIn Learning (https://learning.linkedin.com) and Edx.org offer thousands of courses and micro-certificate programs ranging from business courses, interpersonal skills, to technical courses.

Cost: Just as there are many courses, they also range in cost from no-cost to up to $1,000 per course depending on the faculty, the platform provider, and the specific topic.

Certifications and Skill-Specific Training

Skill Relevance: certifications that validate specific skills will enhance employability and credibility in niche and specialty areas. This may be significant to you if you are taking a career pivot in your Encore Career path. Some professions require certain certifications and a certain number of continuing education units (CEUs) to be completed each year to maintain that certification. Some technology and solution providers create and deliver their own certification courses (i.e. Google, IBM, Salesforce, Meta).

Short-Term Commitment: the relatively short duration of certification programs (on average 4 to 10 weeks) makes them appealing for specific skill enhancement within a limited timeframe.

Cost: Again, there is a wide range of options for certifications and skill training. Costs can vary from $50 to a few thousand dollars depending on the faculty, the platform provider, and the specific topic.

Workshops and Bootcamps

Bootcamps: Bootcamps are intensive, fast-paced training programs, typically designed for those who work in computer science or tech. Over a shortened amount of time, you can learn pivotal skills, like a coding language. If you need to learn the basics on how to code quickly then attending a bootcamp may be a good option. Some bootcamps are offered on site and some are online, depending on the flexibility you need, how self-disciplined you are, and how you learn. Some offer mentors that provide out of class support to learners.

Workshops: Often workshops are short in duration and offer the type of hands-on, practical approaches of learning that foster rapid skill and knowledge acquisition. Further developing the skills and competencies are done afterwards through practice and application.

Cost: Costs vary widely from $50 for a workshop to up to $10,000 for a full bootcamp learning program depending on the faculty, the provider, and the specific topic.

For other ways of learning aside from these formal education options, refer back to the discussion in Chapter 3. Whatever learning path you choose, when you view lifelong learning and education as a continuous journey, you will be better equipped to adapt, grow, and thrive in your Encore Career.

Overcoming Challenges

This section addresses some of the common challenges you may experience when seeking to complete upskilling or reskilling efforts or pursuing further education. Balancing these demands along with existing work and personal commitments may feel intense. This intensity often leads to dropouts or burnout. In the context of preparing for an Encore Career, perhaps we may look at these a bit differently. It may help you to follow some practical strategies such as effective time management, creating a conducive learning environment, and setting realistic goals and expectations.

Balancing Learning with Work and Personal Life

Balancing the pursuit of formal education with existing work and personal commitments is difficult for anyone, and for people in their third act it might make more sense to delay your Encore education journey until after you've finished working in your primary career. If you have the luxury of waiting, we highly recommend it, because there will be more time to dedicate to learning, less stress, and you will be more likely to enjoy the learning process more. If you have a sense of urgency or feel you must push forward, consider these tactics for finding more balance.

Effective time management techniques tailored to the demands of balancing education, work, and personal life:

- Prioritization: identify and prioritize critical tasks and commitments to maximize your time and productivity. It is okay to say 'no' to doing certain things that don't align with the higher level of prioritization.
- Time Blocking: allocate specific blocks of time for learning, for work, and for personal activities to maintain structure. This also helps those around you to know what your availability is relative to all three of these.

Creating a conducive learning environment will help you to stay on track:

- Physical Space: design and dedicate a space for learning that minimizes distractions and promotes focus. If you work from home remotely, you may already have a dedicated workspace.
- Technology and Tools: employ technological tools and software to enhance the learning experience, help you stay on pace with the learning assignments, and improve your efficiency. Ensure you have a strong broadband internet connection, especially if you are working or learning online.

Setting realistic goals and expectations for your education and learning journey is important. Unrealistic goals will be demotivating and may enhance the risk of dropout or burnout:

- Set Achievable Milestones: define what achievable learning milestones are for you based on your life situation and commitments. Then align your learning pace with your personal and Encore Career objectives.
- Flexibility: acknowledge that adjustments may be necessary and that flexibility is key to success. Changing your schedule is not a failure to complete; it is an enabler to completion.

Leverage support systems such as family, friends, and colleagues, to facilitate a smoother balance between education, work, and personal life where possible. Be mindful of your stress levels and practice self-care when needed to reduce stress and maintain overall well-being. It is possible to effectively balance your educational and learning pursuits with work and personal life as you transition into your Encore Career. By prioritizing the most important skills to focus on, determining the ideal way to develop these skills, assessing and prioritizing work and life commitments (if you are still working), creating an optimal learning environment, setting realistic learning goals, leveraging support systems, being mindful of the need for balance and giving yourself some grace, you can confidently navigate a successful and harmonious learning experience while thriving in your third act.

The Power of Networking and Mentoring

Networking and mentorship can play a crucial role in the learning process. The benefits of networking with peers and mentors who can provide guidance, advice, and opportunities for skill development are only as limited as your network. In addition, the new connections you make during the learning process can open doors to new Encore Career prospects.

We already emphasized the power of networking in Chapter 5. Here, we emphasize the pivotal role that networking and mentorship can play in your learning process. Engaging with peers and mentors who can provide guidance, advice, and opportunities for specific skills or competency development could also be a bridge to new Encore Career prospects as well as achieving personal growth goals.

Network connections are ideal for information exchange and discussing industry trends. Networking facilitates the exchange of information, ideas, and experiences, enriching the learning journey. Mentors from your network who have already experienced the transition or pivot to their Encore Career can be a source of professional support, offering insights and guidance, advice, and sharing pitfalls to avoid.

During your learning journey, you will be able to build and expand your peer networks through educational institution forums, online discussion forums, and various social media platforms. These network connections can be valuable sources of motivation, shared knowledge, collaborative learning, and inspiration. On campuses, local learning communities can provide opportunities for face-to-face connections. Alumni associations are also a source for building your network and finding a mentor.

Formal mentors provide guidance, support, and personalized advice that can help accelerate skill development. Mentors can also introduce learners to valuable industry contacts and networking opportunities. To find a suitable mentor consider factors like expertise, availability, and alignment with your Encore Career goals.

As we mentioned in Chapter 5, joining professional organizations and associations related to your Encore Career interests also offers opportunities for networking and mentorship at a deeper, more industry-specific level. These may also lead to Encore Career prospects.

By building your network, leveraging network relationships, finding suitable mentors, and actively participating in learning communities, you are fully harnessing the power of these connections and enriching your learning experiences. Learning is not a one-time event but a lifelong journey. Even if you've neglected your networking efforts before, it is not too late to start. Pursuing your Encore Career makes for an interesting story to share with your network, and your life experiences can help others to learn. By making the effort to share your knowledge as well as learn from them and stay up to date on industry trends, you will be relevant and competitive in your chosen Encore Career.

Speaking of staying relevant, having some knowledge about artificial intelligence (AI) and machine learning (ML) might significantly benefit you. These topics are among the most popular reskilling and continued learning tracks and may be relevant in the context of your Encore Career. Here's how a deeper understanding of AI can enhance your learning and skill development:

- Awareness of AI's Impact on Industries: AI is becoming increasingly prevalent across various industries. Understanding how AI is being adopted and integrated can help you identify the specific skills and knowledge areas that are in demand. This awareness can guide your choices when selecting videos, podcasts, workshops, courses, or certifications to learn more.
- Identifying AI-Related Skill Gaps: Recognizing the growing importance of AI, you may identify gaps in your skill set related to AI technologies. Knowing more about AI allows you to pinpoint these gaps and seek the appropriate learning, education, or training in areas such as machine learning, data analysis, or AI ethics.
- Choosing Relevant AI Courses: With a better understanding of AI, you can make informed decisions when selecting educational options. You can evaluate the content and quality of AI-related courses or programs to ensure you would be gaining valuable skills that align with your Encore Career goals.
- Leveraging AI for Learning: AI-powered tools and platforms are transforming the way people learn. Understanding AI's role in education can help you take full advantage of adaptive learning systems, personalized content recommendations, and AI tutors, making your learning experiences more efficient and effective.
- Anticipating Future Trends: AI is a rapidly evolving field, and staying aware of current trends and emerging technologies can help you anticipate where your industry is heading as it

relates to the use of AI. This knowledge can inform your education and learning priorities to ensure you are acquiring skills that will remain relevant in the near future.

- Interdisciplinary Learning: AI often intersects with various disciplines, such as healthcare, finance, and marketing. Understanding AI's cross-cutting impact enables you to explore interdisciplinary learning opportunities, gaining skills that can be applied in diverse Encore career fields.

In summary, Chapter 7 highlights the importance of upskilling, reskilling, and continuing education in the context of an Encore Career. There are a multitude of ways to learn and selecting the right way of learning for your needs is based on what you want to learn, how you want to learn it, the flexibility you need, and the investment you can make.

<u>CHAPTER 8</u>

Do you want to create a business? If so, you'll need a plan.

But you have to do what you dream of doing even while you're afraid. **—Arianna Huffington**

An entrepreneurial Encore Career is not only a viable option but can also be an exciting and fulfilling one. There are many ways to pursue an entrepreneurial Encore Career such as create a new business, acquire an existing business, join a franchise, join a business partnership, just to name a few. Our focus in this chapter is for those considering creating an entrepreneurial endeavor in their Encore Career. This chapter provides guidance on several important steps including developing a business concept, conducting market research, writing a business plan, and financial and legal implications of starting a business. You will gain the knowledge and tools needed to transform your ideas into a successful business venture.

Developing a Business Concept

The process of conceptualizing and establishing an Encore Career business starts with questioning what aligns with your passions and interests as well as leverages your skills and builds on your knowledge? Using your self-reflections from Chapter 2 would be a good place to start this process. Or you may already have a business idea that resonates with you. Whichever the case may be, we encourage you to consider an Encore Career concept that's both personally meaningful and commercially viable.

- Identify Passions and Interests: Begin by reflecting on your passions and interests. What activities bring you joy and fulfillment? Consider how these elements can be integrated into a business concept. If you already have a business concept in mind, ask yourself how the idea aligns with your passions and interests.
- Skills and Strengths Assessment: Assess your skills and strengths with great honesty. What are you exceptionally

good at? How can you leverage these skills in a business context? If you know that there are areas you will not be good at, then eventually you may want to consider how to resolve those gaps (i.e. Will you need to hire someone? Outsource some of the work? Partner with others who complement your skills?)

Once you've developed your business concept, based on your passions and skills, here are some next steps to get you started on developing your business concept further:

Market Research

Understanding the market is essential for the success of any business. We encourage you to assess the demand, competition, and potential customer base for your business idea. This step is crucial for refining the viability of your business concept and identifying market opportunities.

- Identify Industry Trends: Research current trends and opportunities in the market. Look for gaps or areas where your skills and interests intersect with market demands.
- Target Audience: Define your target audience. Understand their needs, preferences, personas, and pain points. Tailor your business concept to address these aspects, this will help ensure that there is demand for your business.
- Niche Identification: Do you have a highly niche business idea? Explore niche markets where your expertise or specialty can make a unique impact. A specialized focus can set your business apart, differentiate you from others, and attract a specific audience.
- Competitive Analysis: Analyze competitors in your chosen concept or niche. Look at their public information such as websites and other social media. Identify their strengths and weaknesses to find opportunities for differentiation of your own ideas or to fill gaps they may be leaving open.

You've now assessed that your business concept is well aligned with what you are passionate about and the skills that you have, and your market research indicates that there is a need for your business (product, service, solution). These form the foundation of your "why"

- why you are interested in starting this business. Now you can take these to the next step of creating a more detailed viability and sustainability plan explaining your "how" - how you envision bringing it to life.

Business Model

There are a number of models and frameworks available for creating a business model. We suggest you find one that works for you. You can find links to a couple options in the Appendix. The foundation of a business model consists of:

- A company overview (mission and vision)
- A description of your value proposition. (Clearly define the value your business offers to customers. What sets your business apart from others, and why should customers choose you?)
- A synopsis of your target customers
- A description of your brand identity, your brand positioning that clearly communicates the values and personality of your business.
- You may already have ideas for a brand name and logo that you want to get feedback on. (Choose a memorable and relevant business name and design a professional logo that reflects your brand identity.)
- A description of revenue streams. (Determine how your business will generate revenue. Explore different revenue streams, such as product sales, service fees, subscriptions, or a combination.)
- An overview of the competitors and market trends
- An outline of necessary collaborators (i.e. suppliers, sales channels, regulatory requirements, etc.)
- You may want to include an assessment of what impact your business will have on the planet (this could be negative such as resource depletion, pollution, water use, soil use, habitat destruction, greenhouse gas emissions, waste generation, loss of biodiversity; or positive such as the addition of jobs, contributions to local communities, etc.)

The next step is to validate your concept by getting feedback on your business model plan. You may want to ask people you know (friends and family) for their input, as well as from mentors, other business leaders, and network connections. Additionally, it would be ideal if you could get feedback from potential customers - people who fit your 'target audience' as you've defined it. Different ways to gather feedback from others could be through 1:1 conversations, an email campaign, creating a survey, holding informal or formal interviews, or focus groups. By validating there is a genuine need for your product or service, and getting feedback on your business model, you may hear perspectives that you'd not considered. These new perspectives could help you shape your business or give you insights into challenges you may need to consider before moving forward.

If you are creating a new product or new design of a product that already exists, you will want to consider creating a prototype of the product as part of the validation process. Consider developing a Minimum Viable Product (MVP) to test your concept. An MVP is a product, service, solution, or offering with just enough features to validate the idea early in the development cycle, so that potential users can assess it, and you can use their feedback to iterate and refine the product, service, solution, or offering quickly and at little cost.

As you evolve your business model, you will likely be adding a marketing strategy, a sales strategy, and an operational plan. If you need investors, you will most certainly need a financial plan with projections.

Financial Planning and Legal Advice

Depending on what your business idea is, your costs and financial projections can vary. Will you have any startup costs? You will want to estimate what the initial costs will be to start your business. Consider expenses such as supplies, technology, equipment, dedicated space or land, marketing, licenses, and any necessary training. As part of your viability and sustainability plan, you will want to develop financial projections for the first few years. Include estimated income, expenses, and profit margins to assess the financial viability of your business plan.

There are also legal and regulatory considerations when starting a business. For example, what would be the ideal business structure? You will want to choose a legal structure for your business, such as sole proprietorship, LLC, or corporation, which would best suit your short-term and longer-term projections. There will be compliance aspects depending on what legal structure you determine to use. A legal or tax advisor will be able to provide guidance on this decision.

You may also need to consider any business licenses, registrations, and permits related to your business, your industry, your location, and your product(s). Do you need to patent or trademark any part of your business to protect your intellectual property? We highly recommend you speak with a legal professional to ensure you are making the right decisions.

Marketing Strategy

How do you plan on marketing your business? What type of marketing strategy is going to help you to reach your target audience? Will you be using online social media channels and content marketing? Does it make more sense to market your business through offline channels such as networking and in-person demonstrations?

Similar to the techniques we discussed in Chapters 4 and 5, building your personal brand and leveraging your network for job search can translate into actions for your business as well. Having a professional website, getting listed in specific directories, and establishing a search engine optimization (SEO) plan will all help you establish a strong online presence. Leverage digital marketing techniques and artificial intelligence (AI) to reach a broader audience. If you don't know how to do this, there are experts out there who can help you.

By leveraging your professional network or building new connections, you can develop industry connections and relationships with others in your business' focused ecosystem. Networking can lead to valuable partnerships, collaborations, and business opportunities. You may also seek out a mentor who is more experienced in your chosen area of business. Be open to learning from others' insights and experiences. This can help you identify pitfalls to avoid as well as learn what worked well.

Business Growth and Evolution

It is important to remain open to refining your business concept based on feedback and changing market conditions. Your ego can be the greatest deterrent to evolution and adaptability. Your ego is designed to help you make decisions and protect you from harm, but it can also sabotage your ability to hear and accept feedback and take others' perspectives into consideration.

Adaptability is crucial for long-term success. When launching your business you may want to design a pilot launch to test the assumptions and viability of your business model with limited risk. A pilot might be a soft launch with a targeted group or geography that will allow you to test your concept or product on a small scale. This allows you to gather additional feedback and make necessary adjustments before a full-scale launch. This will also give you an idea of the supplies and consumption rate you will need to consider for your longer-term operational plan.

By following these steps, you can systematically develop a business concept that aligns with your Encore Career goals, provides value to customers, and has the potential for long-term success.

In summary, Chapter 8 provided a guide for those of you considering entrepreneurial endeavors in your Encore Career. The steps to develop a business concept, conduct market research, write a compelling business plan, and secure financial and legal advice are important aspects on the route to successful entrepreneurship.

CHAPTER 9
How can I navigate the Encore Career job search?

"Start where you are. Use what you have. Do what you can."
—Arthur Ashe

If starting your own business does not interest you, then perhaps your Encore Career will be more aligned with becoming a freelancer, working on contract or on a project basis, or perhaps a steady part-time job is more aligned with what your Encore Career goals are. Whatever type of meaningful and purposeful work you identified in Chapters 2 and 3, this chapter will help you identify how to leverage your skills and expertise in your new Encore Career direction. Remember, you've already done a lot of the hard work to identify what you want to do, what you are good at, and established Encore Career goals that align with your values in Chapter 2. In Chapter 3 you assessed industry trends and took stock of your personal circumstances to determine the direction of your Encore Career. Now it's time to put all these pieces together.

Depending on how different your career ideas were in Chapters 2 and 3, it is likely these next steps will require a career pivot or a transition from what your primary career was. You may recall from Chapter 4 the discussion about maintaining a growth mindset and the strategies to embrace change in order to exhibit adaptability - which is an important element in pursuing your Encore Career.

This chapter is intended to empower you to navigate the job search and enable you to find the type of work that will fulfill your Encore Career goals. In this chapter you will be guided through the job search process with a focus on identifying jobs that align with your Encore Career goals. If you've not looked for a job in a while you may be surprised to find out how different job search is now. We'll start with a discussion on crafting a compelling narrative that will help you tell your story about why you are making the transition.

You will need to create or revise a resume that emphasizes your transferable skills, and we will discuss the importance of a cover letter that can help others understand your motivation for making a career transition. Speaking of others, leveraging your professional network (our discussion in Chapter 5) during job search is going to be a key contributor to finding what you are looking for. This chapter will also provide tips on how to prepare for interviews, how to evaluate jobs and companies to ensure they are a good fit for you, and the best ways to negotiate for the salary offers you deserve.

Getting Comfortable With Change and Uncertainty

Pursuing something new in your Encore Career, or even tangential to your primary career, requires a shift in your mindset and change to your job search approach. Whether you are pursuing a new career path, looking to become a volunteer, or exploring new areas of interest, you will likely be facing some challenges and uncertainty. It is good to be open minded and accept this upfront. In fact, you may already be feeling some discomfort about the uncertainty of what lies ahead. This is very natural, especially if your primary career followed a predictable path.

The transitions you will be facing as you pursue your Encore Career goals can be opportunities for growth and learning. Staying curious can help you feel more comfortable with ambiguity and uncertainty. You can't expect to know everything, and you will become disappointed and frustrated if you have too many expectations and things don't always go the way you'd planned. Remaining flexible and open to new possibilities is critical to enjoying the journey.

As we've discussed in Chapters 6 and 7, you will likely be navigating personal and professional changes as you pursue your Encore Career. These may include:

- changes in family and relationship dynamics
- building new connections in your network
- adapting to financial and income changes
- potentially exploring new types of work, new industries

- adapting to new technology
- learning new skills

By viewing change as an opportunity for growth, you will build your natural resiliency and develop new ways to cope with challenges, uncertainty, and setbacks. Adopting a growth mindset and remaining open to modifying your goals or your timeline in response to new opportunities or challenges will allow you to more easily adapt and become more comfortable with being uncomfortable.

Getting Started

One of the first steps in preparing for your job search is crafting your compelling narrative. This is an essential component when transitioning to an Encore Career. Your narrative should effectively communicate why you're making the transition, highlight your transferable skills, and showcase your motivation for pursuing this new path. Following along with your narrative, your resume and any branding (such as your LinkedIn profile) should align with the narrative about your new Encore Career direction.

Here are key elements to consider:

Understand Your Why and Create Your Narrative: Review your earlier self-flections of your passions and interests from Chapter 2 and reflect on the reasons behind your career transition. Your narrative will explain what motivated you to pursue an Encore Career and why you've chosen to pursue "X". You will explain how "X" will provide personal fulfillment, allow you to follow your passion for a new industry, or enable you to make a meaningful impact, for example. Being able to express your why will help inform others as to your intentions of pursuing your Encore Career. Practice your narrative so that you become very comfortable with it. It should begin to flow naturally and feel conversational.

Identify Your Relevant Transferable Skills: Review your professional experience and identify transferable skills that are relevant to your desired Encore Career roles. Transferable skills are ones that can be applied in a multitude of situations and are not specific to a certain company or certain job. These may include, for example, leadership capabilities, problem-solving skills, communication expertise, project management experience. Consider what skills are needed in the role you are pursuing. Then tailor your narrative to highlight these transferable skills in a way that will resonate with people in your target industry.

Not sure what skills are needed? You may want to start by conducting a job title search for roles that reflect the type of work you wish to pursue. Then take a look at the descriptions for the qualifications, expectations, and identifiable skills. This will help you to consider which technical or functional skills to emphasize on your resume as well.

Craft Your Resume: You may want to consider using a functional or hybrid resume format that is designed to focus on skills and competencies rather than chronological work history and job titles. This is especially true if you are making a significant career pivot or transitioning to a new industry. Revise your resume to emphasize your transferable skills and showcase your suitability for your desired Encore Career role. Whenever possible, use quantifiable achievements and concrete examples to demonstrate your related capabilities. Use numbers, percentages, or other metrics to quantify the results of your actions and highlight your contributions in previous roles.

Create a "Skills and Competencies" section dedicated at the top of your resume to listing your relevant transferable skills to make it easier for employers to identify relevant abilities. Remember to also showcase any relevant training, courses, or certifications you've completed especially as you worked through Chapter 7 to close any knowledge gaps for your target Encore Career role. Completing these demonstrates your commitment to continuous learning and skill development as well as being current in your desired field. If you are unfamiliar with writing or revising a resume, there are professional resume writers for hire as well as templates and online resources available to assist you.

If you are pursuing contract, consulting, or gig work, rather than a standard resume, you may want to create more of a one-page marketing flier outlining the services you provide. You would save the flier as a pdf so it could easily be shared as an attachment to an email.

There are many templates and designs available online for this type of document.

Modify Your LinkedIn Profile: Review the sections in Chapters 3 and 4 about creating your new brand that is aligned with your Encore Career pursuits. Use your LinkedIn profile headline area and emphasize the relevant transferable skills so that people know what you are moving towards and the desired roles you are pursuing. You can set your profile as "Open To Work" so that recruiters will know that you are actively pursuing new opportunities. Within this profile setting you can specify the job titles, locations, work arrangement preferences (onsite, hybrid, or remote) so recruiters can assess if you could be a good candidate for their vacancies.

If you are pursuing contract, consulting, or gig work, you can use your LinkedIn profile to indicate that you are "Providing Services". You may want to invest in a LinkedIn Premium Business subscription. This will allow you to include media and features about your services in a carousel, add a "Request Proposal" button, provide a preview of your service description, and allow people to rate your services. To begin offering your services on LinkedIn, you'll need to create a LinkedIn Service Page. LinkedIn Service Pages are dedicated landing pages that showcase your services and businesses at no cost and enable you to be found through searches people conduct on LinkedIn.

Write a Compelling Cover Letter: Some people may advise against using a cover letter, with the assumption that recruiters rarely read them, so they are a waste of time. However, your cover letter will provide a critical opportunity to narrate your career transition story in detail and help bridge an understanding of why you are pursuing a role that is different from your past experience. Use the cover letter to explain your motivation for transitioning, why you're passionate about the new industry or role, and how your skills and experience align with the position you're applying for. Be authentic and sincere in conveying your enthusiasm and commitment to your chosen new career path. A cover letter doesn't need to be longer than those three paragraphs. Any longer than that and it could be detrimental to your effort.

Leverage Your Professional Network

Throughout this book we have mentioned that your professional network is a valuable tool in your tool box when building your Encore Career. This is especially true during a job search, and especially when transitioning to a new career direction. Even if you've previously neglected to build your LinkedIn professional network, it is not too late to reach out to people with whom you have worked in the past to connect with them now. Not everyone is active on LinkedIn, but once you connect you will have access to their email address. Reach out to connections in your professional network who may offer insights, advice, and very importantly they can let you know about any job opportunities related to your Encore Career goals. You can also use LinkedIn to expand your network and connect with like-minded professionals already established in the area you wish to pursue or working at companies you'd like to target for your job search.

Aim to share your narrative with a few trusted connections and ask for feedback to help you continue to hone your story. You may want to do this before you start to speak with recruiters. You may also want to attend industry events, join and participate in relevant online communities. These are great places to introduce yourself and practice your new Encore Career direction narrative.

Job Boards

Several job boards cater specifically to individuals seeking Encore Career opportunities, which list jobs that are typically geared towards flexible, meaningful work opportunities. Some job boards have fees associated with searching their job listings. Be sure to assess their relevance for the types of jobs you are seeking before paying for access. Online job boards, as well as Google for Jobs, often allow you to set alerts so they will send you an email or text to let you know about new job listings that you may be interested in based on your search criteria. You may find local job boards in your city that have been developed specifically for job seekers who are over 50. Below are a few national job boards that might also be useful for searching specifically for Encore Career roles:

RetirementJobs.com: RetirementJobs.com is a job board specifically designed for people over 50 who are transitioning into retirement or seeking part-time and flexible work opportunities. It features job listings from a wide range of industries and allows users to search for roles based on location, industry, and job type.

FlexJobs.com: FlexJobs is a popular job board that specializes in remote and flexible work opportunities. While not exclusively focused on Encore Careers, FlexJobs features a variety of part-time, freelance, and remote positions that may be suitable for individuals looking to transition into a new career phase.

AARP.com Job Board: The AARP Job Board offers a range of job listings targeted towards older adults, including encore career opportunities. It features full-time, part-time, and temporary roles across different industries and allows users to search for jobs based on location and job category.

Workforce50.com: Workforce50 is a job board that focuses on helping individuals over 50 find employment opportunities. It features job listings from companies that value experienced workers and offers resources and articles to support older adults in their job search.

Evaluate Companies and Job Opportunities

When evaluating job opportunities, consider factors such as company culture and alignment with your values and priorities. Is it a fast-paced, competitive work environment? Will they expect you to work long hours? Is this what you are looking for at this stage in your career? Look beyond job titles and salary when evaluating opportunities. Consider factors such as the company strategy, their mission, and the company's growth potential. You can find a lot of this information on the company website and on other sites that rank company reputation. Even if the job seems perfect, be sure to research prospective employers thoroughly, including what employees say about them, their financial stability, recent news-worthy stories about them, social media posts, and even customer reviews to determine if you wish to be a part of their company. Perhaps you know a current or former employee and can get firsthand insights into the organizational culture. Ask about their experiences, what they enjoy most about working for the company, and any challenges they encountered.

Consider the leadership style within the organization and how it may impact your experience as an employee. Look for evidence of transparent communication, mentorship opportunities, and a supportive leadership team that values employee development. Evaluate the dynamics of the teams you'll be working with and how they align with your working style and preferences. Consider factors such as collaboration, communication, and team cohesion.

Does the company publicize any cultural initiatives or community programs they engage with? Look for signs of employee engagement and satisfaction within the organization. Employee reviews and testimonials can provide insights into how employees perceive the company culture, their level of job satisfaction, and any challenges they face. Assess the company's approach to work-life balance and whether it aligns with your personal preferences and priorities. Look for information about flexible work arrangements, remote work options, and employee wellness programs. Assess the company's commitment to promoting a diverse and inclusive workplace. Look for evidence of diverse representation at all levels of the organization and inclusive policies and practices.

Prepare for Interviews

When you do get a recruiter reaching out to you, they will probably ask to set up a phone interview. Anticipate questions about your career transition during interviews and prepare thoughtful responses that highlight your strengths, skills, and enthusiasm for the new role. Practice articulating your career narrative in a concise and compelling manner, emphasizing how your past experiences combined with your passions and interests have prepared you for success in the role you applied for. Be prepared to discuss your resume and work history in detail. Review your past experiences, accomplishments, and key projects or achievements. Be ready to provide examples that illustrate your skills, strengths, and contributions.

In addition, research common interview questions for your target industry and role - these can often be found online. Prepare responses to common interview questions, such as "Tell me about yourself," "Why are you interested in this position?" and "What are your strengths and weaknesses?" Practice your answers aloud to ensure clarity and coherence. Practice your responses, focusing on how your skills and experiences relate to the requirements of the role. Develop concise and compelling stories that highlight your achievements, problem-solving abilities, and adaptability. You may want to use the STAR format (situation, task, action, result) to answer behavioral interview questions that are designed to reveal how you behave in certain situations.

If you get to interview with the hiring manager and other potential colleagues, be sure you understand the job description, review the key responsibilities, required skills, and qualifications. Identify specific examples from your experience that demonstrate your ability to meet these requirements. Be prepared to discuss how your skills and experience align with the job requirements. Practice active listening and prepare thoughtful questions to ask the interviewers about the company culture, team dynamics, and other questions about the company that will help you to determine if it is a good fit for your next career move. You might ask the interviewer about the company, the role, the team dynamics, or any other relevant topics. Asking thoughtful questions demonstrates your interest in the position and the company and can help you gather important information to make an informed decision.

If you have a video interview, which is very common now, expect to have your camera on and dress appropriately even though you will not be in person. Be aware of what is behind you on the video and ensure you have proper lighting and enough battery power or plug in your computer. You definitely would not want your computer battery to die in the middle of an interview.

Pay attention to your body language, tone of voice, and facial expressions during the interview. Practice maintaining good posture, making eye contact, and using confident, friendly gestures. These are, of course, also relevant if you will be going into the company's place of business for an interview. Choose professional attire that aligns with the company culture and industry norms. Dressing appropriately demonstrates your professionalism and respect for the interview process.

Trust your instincts and intuition when evaluating organizational culture fit. Pay attention to your gut feeling during the interview process and consider whether you feel comfortable and aligned with the company's culture and values. Assess whether the role and organization align with your Encore Career goals and aspirations and will provide meaningful and purposeful work that align with your interests.

Follow-up after the interviews and send a thank-you email, or handwritten note, to the interviewer within 24-48 hours after the interview. Express your gratitude for the opportunity, reiterate your interest in the position, and briefly summarize why you are a strong candidate for the role.

Just to manage your expectations, it is unfortunate, but many companies use automated emails to notify candidates that they have not been selected after applying and after interviewing. This does not offer much opportunity for getting feedback on how you can improve your interviewing or why you were not selected.

Negotiating Job Offers

Compensation approaches and philosophies differ greatly across industries. The first step in negotiating salary offers is to research salary benchmarks for your desired role so you know what to expect. Understanding what you can ask for will give you the confidence to ask for fair and equitable compensation. Research salary ranges for similar roles in your target industry and geographic location using online resources and salary surveys. Websites like Glassdoor, PayScale, and LinkedIn Salary can provide valuable insights into salary ranges for your position. Use this information to establish a reasonable salary range based on your qualifications and experience.

> Recruiters will often ask what your salary expectations are in the initial interview, so be prepared to ask them for the salary range rather than providing one to them. Assess if their salary range

matches your expectations. Savvy negotiators ask for more than they are willing to accept at the start of the negotiations. By asking for slightly more than your ideal salary you are giving yourself room for negotiation. This allows you to make concessions during the negotiation process while still achieving a satisfactory outcome. Confidence in your worth will strengthen your negotiating position. When negotiating a salary offer, emphasize the value you bring to the role and be prepared to advocate for yourself confidently. Understand your own value and the unique skills and experience you bring to the table. Be prepared to articulate the specific ways you can contribute to the company's success or have a positive impact on their business.

When negotiating a job offer, use confident and assertive language, and avoid apologizing or downplaying your worth. Be open to negotiation and compromise. The company may have budget constraints or other factors that may influence their ability to offer a higher salary. Look for ways to find a mutually beneficial solution. You might wait until you have a formal job offer before initiating salary discussions.

You can accept a verbal offer, but once you've reached an agreement, be sure to get the final offer in writing and that it includes all terms carefully discussed. Once you have an offer in hand, you have more leverage to negotiate. Consider negotiating other aspects of a job offer besides base pay, such as variable bonuses, paid time off, benefits, flexible work arrangements, and professional development opportunities, depending on what is important to you. Sometimes, negotiating non-salary components can be just as valuable as negotiating salary.

Be prepared to walk away if the company is unwilling to meet your salary expectations. Remember that your time and skills are valuable, and it's essential to work for a company that respects and values your contributions.

There are many online resources with career tips, job-search tools, and advice. For experienced workers looking for roles more aligned with their Encore Career, we suggest checking out the AARP.org/work section. You may find that these resources are more tailored to your needs and provide career resources and articles on topics related to Encore Careers and age-friendly workplaces.

In summary, this chapter provided a guide on how to navigate your Encore Career job search and enable you to find the type of work that will fulfill your Encore Career goals. Being clear on what you are good at, what you want to do, and who you wish to do it with will help you craft a compelling narrative that tells why you are making the transition into your Encore Career. Leveraging your professional network, searching job boards, and evaluating jobs and companies to ensure they are a good fit for you are the next steps. Preparing well for interviews and negotiating the best salary offer will ensure you land in a place that fits your Encore Career desire and are compensated appropriately.

<u>CHAPTER 10</u>

Ready to launch your Encore Career!?!

"As long as you keep going, you'll keep getting better. And as you get better, you gain more confidence. That alone is success." **—Tamara Taylor**

Well, at this point you pretty much know everything you need to know about getting started on your Encore Career. Are you ready to take the leap? It may feel scary, or you may be feeling completely ready. This chapter is designed to motivate you to take action on your Encore Career goals and overcome any remaining fears or doubts. In this chapter we will address some common initial challenges you may face and provide tips on how to stay committed to your journey.

Overcoming Fear and Doubt: Embracing Your Encore Career with Confidence

Whether it's the fear of the unknown, financial concerns, or self-doubt, it is quite natural to still be feeling a bit hesitant to get started. Recognizing these common fears and doubts will allow you to address them and hopefully overcome them. Others before you have faced similar fears and doubts and have successfully navigated through them. Hearing about the experiences of others and learning from their experiences can be a source of inspiration and motivation.

Setting Realistic Expectations

It's crucial for you to set realistic expectations about the early stages of your Encore Career. Success may take time and patience, and initial setbacks are part of the learning process. Managing expectations can help you stay resilient in the face of challenges.

If you've been wildly or even mildly successful in your primary career, then you may become frustrated with the pace at which your Encore Career takes off. Managing this impatience may be challenging at times. Remember that pursuing your Encore Career is a journey, not a destination. There will be ups and downs, but each experience, even setbacks, contributes to personal and professional growth. Staying committed and flexible, especially in the early stages, is crucial to your success.

Avoid hasty decisions or the urge to give up. Having patience may prevent you from making impulsive career decisions you may regret later. If you know that you are the type of person who might fall into this pitfall, you may want to ask a trusted friend or relative to always be available to talk with you when you find yourself in this mindset.

Managing your emotional responses to challenges can be difficult. Coping with the frustration in a healthy manner such as ensuring you have a balanced diet, getting enough sleep, and maintaining a dose of positivity each day can help. Maintaining positivity and optimism especially during the early stages of an Encore Career is key to staying committed.

Remember, it is okay to lean on others when things get tough. Family, friends, mentors, peers, and professional network connections can help you gain or regain perspective and provide guidance during challenging times. Sometimes you just need an empathetic listener, other times you need specific advice. Surround yourself with a support system to provide you with what you need when you need it.

Keeping a long-term perspective sometimes helps to see the bigger picture. The early stages of your Encore Career are just one part of a more extensive journey. Your Encore Career goals may also evolve and change over time, leading to new and exciting opportunities.

Celebrating Small Victories

At the beginning, even the smallest accomplishments should be celebrated in some way. Continuing to recognize your progress and acknowledging and celebrating both small achievements and major milestones can boost your morale and motivation. This is why it is important to build some milestones into your plan. The celebration doesn't have to be big and loud, it can be as simple as a quiet conversation with someone to share what you've accomplished.

Remember that you cannot anticipate or plan for everything, so we must learn from all our experiences, successes, and setbacks. See these as stepping stones to future success. Acknowledging these achievements can serve as a significant driver of motivation. Small victories contribute to building confidence. Each success, no matter how modest, boosts your belief in your abilities and capacity to achieve your Encore Career aspirations. As confidence grows, so does motivation. Confident individuals are more likely to take on new challenges, pursue ambitious goals, and maintain a positive attitude, all of which are crucial in an Encore Career.

Sharing your successes with others can be an additional motivator. By celebrating achievements openly, you receive support and recognition from your network, whether it's friends, family, or professional contacts. This external validation can boost your motivation and create a sense of accountability. Knowing that others are invested in your success can further inspire you to stay committed to your career goals. You also allow those who are helping you to feel good about their contributions to your achievements.

Celebrating small victories is not just a momentary feel-good exercise; it's a vital source of motivation in pursuit of an Encore Career. By recognizing progress, building confidence, and embracing personal growth as a form of celebration, you can be more motivated and committed to achieving your goals.

The Role of Gratitude

An attitude of gratitude can help you appreciate the journey you are on and find joy in the process. Gratitude breeds positivity and strengthens resilience. Showing gratitude to the people who have helped you and are helping you on your journey is important. Gratitude can be a powerful tool in the process of celebrating small victories and maintaining motivation in your Encore Career.

Gratitude involves acknowledging the value of the path you've chosen and recognizing the positive aspects of the experience. Gratitude prompts you to reflect on your progress and encourages you to focus on what you have achieved rather than dwelling on what's yet to be accomplished. Gratitude can help you find joy in the process of pursuing your Encore Career by shifting the focus from the end goal to the daily steps you've taken, fostering a sense of contentment and fulfillment along the way. Gratitude also allows you to embrace the challenges and setbacks you encounter in your Encore Career as opportunities for growth and learning rather than obstacles.

When you express gratitude it fosters a positive mindset and literally impacts both physiological and psychological changes in your body. These include reduced cortisol levels which reduces stress, increased levels of oxytocin which encourages feelings of love, increased levels of endorphins which are natural opioids associated with pain relief, lower blood pressure and heart rate, promotes improved sleep, reduces anxiety and depression, fosters better blood sugar control, and overall reduces the risk of poor health. This is how gratitude creates more positivity and can help you to stay focused, motivated, maintain a can-do attitude, and facing any challenges with a constructive outlook.

Staying Committed to Your Encore Career Journey

This may be another good time to remind you that the Encore Career journey is more like a marathon than a sprint. Motivation and goal setting are vital aspects of commitment. Setting clear, achievable, and personally meaningful goals provides you with direction and motivation. Regularly revisiting your goals helps you stay on track and measure your progress. Celebrating small victories along the way can fuel your motivation.

Your support system plays a crucial role in commitment. Share your journey with your support network, and let them help you stay dedicated to your goals. They can offer encouragement, accountability, and assistance when needed. They will appreciate you keeping them informed of your progress.

Focusing on your purpose is another way to stay committed. Remind yourself of the reasons you embarked on your Encore Career journey. Reconnecting with your sense of purpose can reignite your commitment when it wavers. You may want to write your purpose statement on a post-it note and put it somewhere that you will see it frequently as a reminder.

Taking care of yourself and maintaining a work-life balance is essential. Overcommitting and neglecting your well-being can lead to burnout. Ensuring you allocate time for relaxation, hobbies, and self-care helps you stay energized and committed to your goals.

When setbacks occur, it's essential to view them as learning opportunities. Reflect on what went wrong, identify areas for improvement, and adjust your approach accordingly. This proactive response to challenges reinforces your commitment to the journey.

Keep the bigger picture in mind. Your Encore Career is part of a larger plan for personal fulfillment and continued growth. When faced with challenges, consider how they fit into the broader narrative of your life and career.

Measuring Success Beyond Financial Gain

Success in an Encore Career is not solely measured by financial gain. You've been encouraged throughout this book to define your criteria for success, which may include personal fulfillment, the impact you will make, or the joy you will derive from your work. Shifting the focus from financial rewards to holistic well-being can be liberating and motivating. In your Encore Career you will not have the constraints of traditional career success measures and therefore perhaps can find greater motivation and satisfaction.

Seeking personal fulfillment is a fundamental aspect of success in an Encore Career. Reflect back to the earlier chapters where you explored what truly fulfills you. What impact and contribution do you wish to make? Success in an Encore Career can be gauged by the impact and contribution you make to your communities, causes, or fields of choice. Reflect on the difference you wish to make through your work and how it aligns with your values and goals. The sense of purpose derived from making a meaningful impact can be a powerful indicator of success.

Finding joy and passion in one's work is another significant aspect of success. Reflect back to when you were considering what joy your

Encore Career would bring you, what ignited your passion for this pursuit? Genuine enjoyment can be a powerful driving force in an Encore Career.

Achieving true work-life balance can be a measure of success. Achieving balance and maintaining one's well-being while pursuing an Encore Career is a significant accomplishment. Evaluate how well you are managing the demands of starting your Encore career alongside enjoying your personal life.

Are you continuing to grow and learn from the experience? Success can also be taking the journey itself, marked by a willingness to adapt, acquiring new skills, and exploring new interests. The courage you are portraying can be a fulfilling measure of success.

Consider the legacy and impact you are creating through your Encore Career. The impact you have on others, whether through mentoring, knowledge sharing, or inspiration, can also be a meaningful gauge of success.

Taking the Leap: Embracing Your Encore Career Journey

This is a culmination of your preparation and self-reflection, you are now ready to embrace your Encore Career journey with enthusiasm and determination. You are encouraged to relieve your fears and overcome any doubts, it is time to step into your Encore Career with confidence and purpose. Here are a few additional thoughts to ponder:

Life is short. Time and life are finite, and time is a precious resource. Don't postpone your dreams and passions, instead seize the opportunity to create a fulfilling Encore Career. Make the most of the present moment.

Pursue your passions. No matter whose plan you were pursuing during your primary career, you have now had the opportunity to explore your personal passions and interests. Pursuing an Encore Career is an opportunity to follow one's heart and engage in work that aligns with your true desires and one that truly resonates with you.

Make a difference. In your Encore Career you have the potential to make a meaningful impact in your chosen field or community. Consider how your skills, experience, and passions will contribute to positive change and bring about a sense of purpose. The prospect of leaving a legacy and making a difference can be a compelling motivator.

Embrace being uncomfortable. Taking the leap often involves stepping out of one's comfort zone. New beginnings can be uncomfortable and challenging, but personal growth and transformation often occur outside of one's comfort zone. Embrace the discomfort as a sign of growth and development.

Build your confidence. Confidence is a key factor in taking the leap. We have provided you with many strategies for building self-confidence, including setting realistic expectations, focusing on past achievements, and seeking support and feedback. Confidence is a tool for conquering fears and pursuing an Encore Career with assurance.

Believe in yourself. Your beliefs and your mindset play a crucial role in your success. By cultivating a positive belief in your abilities and believing in the potential of your Encore Career, you are more likely to overcome obstacles, stay on the path, and achieve your goals.

Embrace opportunities. Be open to opportunities and do not be deterred by potential setbacks or failures. Your Encore Career journey will be filled with many chances to learn and grow. See challenges as opportunities for personal and professional development.

In summary, "Take the Leap"! Chapter 10 has been more of a motivational guide to encourage you to move forward and begin the transition into your Encore Career. There will always be fears and doubts, but by setting realistic expectations, redefining success, celebrating small victories, and building a strong support system you can begin to take action, stay committed to your goals, and embark on the fulfilling journey of your Encore Career.

CHAPTER 11

Remember to balance work and life.

"Our daily decisions and habits have a huge impact upon both our levels of happiness and success." **—Shawn Achor**

Maintaining a healthy work-life balance is essential for the sustainability of an Encore Career. In this chapter, we will cover strategies for staying healthy, reducing stress, nurturing relationships with family and friends, and pursuing hobbies and passions outside of work. All these areas are crucial parts of achieving the feeling of balance you want in your Encore Career. We encourage you to create a plan for overall well-being during your career transition and here we offer ways you can achieve it.

The Importance of Work Life Harmony

Did you feel that you were able to achieve the elusive "work-life balance" during your primary career? If so, then you deserve a hearty congratulations, because many people do not feel this way. Most adults who work full-time and are also managing other obligations often feel overwhelmed. Realistically, the act of balancing work and life is a constantly changing challenge because life is constantly changing. Striving for a harmonic sense of work and life may be more achievable, but it still requires intentional orchestration.

One of the keys to achieving any kind of harmony between work and life at any time in your career is to define what that means for you personally and control as much of the situation as you can. Figuring out your priorities and what you want to be spending your time on is a part of this. Since everyone's situation is unique - work is different, and everyone's life and obligations are different - there cannot be a one-size fits all approach to achieving work-life harmony.

This holds true for achieving some sense of balance in your Encore Career. While you transition into your next chapter in life, where pursuing meaningful work is a central goal, let's proactively ensure that it does not come at the expense of personal health, relationships, and overall well-being. Achieving a feeling of work life harmony, based on your personal definition of what that is, is about how you choose to spend your time. This is essential for Encore Career sustainability.

Managing Your Time Effectively

You may have tried many different time management techniques in your past and attempted to set clear boundaries between work and personal life. When it comes to your Encore Career, you will have more control over your time and this includes prioritizing tasks, eliminating time-wasting activities, and ensuring that work does not encroach on personal time.

You have the opportunity in your Encore Career to choose what you want to spend your time doing! As you consider the many things you want to be doing, consider also how you will ensure that your time is used efficiently.

<u>Prioritizing Tasks and Activities:</u>

- Use To-Do Lists: The benefits of creating daily or weekly to-do lists are that they help you to organize and prioritize tasks that have to get done.
- Urgent vs. Important: Distinguishing between urgent tasks and important tasks will help you to allocate your time accordingly.

One common method for organizing and prioritizing your To Do's based on what is urgent and important is through the Eisenhower Matrix. Challenge yourself to use this 2 x 2 matrix (as shown below) to list all of your tasks in the boxes marked either urgent/not urgent and important/not important. Next, be sure to allocate the appropriate amount of time to what is in the urgent and important box, while taking action on the other boxes as appropriate. Keep in mind also that others may have a different perspective of what is urgent and important than your own view, so it is a good idea to share your matrix with your partner or anyone else who is depending on you for a task.

Eisenhower Time Management Matrix

	URGENT	LESS URGENT
IMPORTANT	(1) Do These First First focus on these important tasks that need to be done with more immediacy.	(2) Decide on These Decide how/when to do these important tasks that can be scheduled.
LESS IMPORTANT	(3) Delegate These These are the tasks that are urgent but are less important and can be done by others.	(4) Delete These or Don't Do Them These are tasks that are neither urgent nor important, so don't do them at all, or at least minimize these.

Setting Boundaries

When trying to establish balance, determine what the ideal integration of work and life looks like for you. Identify your core needs, make the decision to incorporate them as priorities into your schedule, and keep some flexibility in mind as things change.

The areas that help keep you going every week and make you feel balanced and whole will sustain you throughout your Encore Career. Once you know what matters most, you can work on setting boundaries around those activities so that whether you're at work or elsewhere, you can be more fully present for those around you.

Whatever matters most to you, make a list and figure out which items are negotiable and which aren't. When you have a more complete picture of what you're willing to flex on, you can work toward better integration of your work and life priorities.

Below are a few ideas that may help you to establish clearer boundaries and achieve more balance between your work and personal life:

- Designated workspaces: Creating a designated workspace for work-related activities to maintain a boundary between professional and personal spaces. This is especially important if you frequently conduct work activities from home.
- Time-Blocking and scheduled breaks: Time-blocking for dedicated work hours to ensure focused productivity, along

with scheduled breaks can help prevent work from encroaching on personal time. Time-blocking for personal and leisure activities is very important to maintaining a work-life balance as well. You are more likely to stick to a commitment to yourself or to others when you've made plans.

- Eliminate time-wasting activities: Identify the types of things that drain your time. Go back and review the 2x2 priority matrix and be sure you are not spending too much time doing things in the bottom-right quadrant (less important/less urgent). These activities may consume your time without adding much value to your personal or professional life.
- Streamline tasks: Whenever possible, consider workflows and alternative ways of doing things that can help you reduce the time you spend doing them. Try the 'touch it once' approach - whether it's a text, an email, a report to review, or something to file, the idea is that as soon as you touch something, you complete that task or determine the next steps to move the task forward. By taking care of something right away instead of saving it and going back to it at a later time, you've taken a more decisive action and eliminated wasted time in your day.
- Avoid multitasking: You may think you are a master multitasker, but studies show that multitasking actually reduces productivity. It is much more effective to focus on completing one task at a time for maximum efficiency.
- Maximize the use of technology: Using a scheduler and calendar reminders can help you improve your time management, especially if you often tend to lose track of time. You may find that the use of apps on your phone and tools on your desktop that are designed to help you stay organized are helpful.
- Avoid time-consuming tasks: Checking your phone, texts, emails constantly throughout the day requires a lot of your time. Try checking these only at certain times of the day. Turn off your notifications and ringers, and leave your phone on vibrate to create these 'quiet times'.
- Try saying "no" to things that do not align with your purpose and your priorities: Your ability to say "no" to things is a

learned skill and may require you to overcome the fear of missing out (FOMO). When you are not able to say "no", then you may be saying "yes" to things that are inconsequential to your goals and may take away time from your priorities. Sometimes the inability to say "no" ends up with you taking on too much commitment. Being clear on your purpose, values, and priorities can empower you to say "no, thank you".

- Setting boundaries with others: Whether it is your family, clients, your employer, or friends, setting boundaries with others regarding your availability will ensure you maintain control over your time. This may feel challenging at first, but keep at it, because it is quite empowering once you get the hang of it.

Nurturing Relationships

Even though we just shared the importance of setting boundaries to avoid other people from encroaching on your work life balance, it is equally important to still nurture your relationships. Yes, you read that right! Personal relationships can become strained when you are making a change in your priorities, as often occurs when one is pursuing an Encore Career. Depending on the demands of your chosen path, you may have less time for certain aspects of your life. However, nurturing family and social connections, maintaining open communication, and ensuring that relationships remain a source of support and fulfillment are important to help you feel successful.

Throughout these chapters, we've discussed the importance of managing your own and other people's expectations. Establishing open communication about what you are doing with people in your life that are important to you can help you to engage them in the process of pursuing your Encore Career. These are the people who believe in you, who encourage you, and will support you. Remember to make the time to spend with these loved ones and friends. Also, be aware of managing your stress and the emotional investment involved with career transitions as these may inadvertently affect your personal connections.

By sharing your plans and your Encore Career goals, motivations, and the expected time commitments with family and friends, you can help them understand how your availability could be changing. Be open to hearing their perspectives and any concerns expressed by family members and friends, and be respectful of their opinions. Show appreciation and gratitude for their interest, whether you agree with them or not.

Sometimes it helps to set priorities around family time and social time to help better manage the family's expectations and their needs. Explain to them that you need them for emotional support, especially during a challenging career transition. Talk about the expectation of mutual support and the encouragement you can provide them as well. Discuss with them the importance of quality time over quantity of time.

Staying Physically and Emotionally Healthy

Physical and emotional health are cornerstones of wellbeing. Choosing a healthy lifestyle includes maintaining strong interpersonal relationships as well as regular exercise, a balanced diet, and adequate sleep. Some people find it helpful to use stress management techniques, such as meditation, mindfulness, and relaxation exercises to help cope with the challenges of establishing an Encore Careers.

There is a strong connection between health, wellbeing, and achieving a sense of work-life harmony. Physical vitality directly impacts your energy levels, mobility, strength, and the ability to fully enjoy life. Emotional strength and resilience enhances your capacity to manage stress and maintain a sense of mental wellbeing.

- Exercise: Setting aside time for regular exercise is imperative for wellbeing. We don't mean that you should be training for a marathon, but even just 30-minutes a day to incorporate a routine of walking, jumping, and strength training can significantly improve both your physical and emotional wellbeing.
- Nourishment: By this time in your life, you are probably well aware of nutrition basics, so we don't need to harp on the fact that eating a healthy diet of lean proteins and colorful vegetables is important. It is amazing how well you will feel if you limit fatty foods and alcohol, minimize eating processed foods, and reduce your sugar intake. Meal planning and

intentionally eating healthy with a partner can help you stick to a nutritious diet. If you dislike meal prepping or cooking for yourself, there are convenient meal plans you can sign up for online, you can order what you enjoy eating, and have it shipped directly to your house.

- Prioritize Adequate Sleep: As we age, some people find it more difficult to get a good night's rest. You may find it harder to fall asleep, you may wake up more often during the night, or you may find that you are awakening earlier in the morning. How much sleep you need is an individual thing, but aim for 6.5 to 7 hours per night. Be sure you have a comfortable sleeping environment (no loud noise, slightly cool temperature, minimum light) and focus on your quality of sleep rather than over-worry about quantity (over-worrying can create a cycle of anxiety that will likely prevent you from getting a good night of sleep).
- Manage Stress: We all have stress, and some people are able to manage it better than others. Choosing a stress management technique that works for you is an important part of achieving emotional well-being. Meditation, breathing exercises, mindfulness activities, and relaxation exercises such as yin yoga are common practices for managing and alleviating stress.

By intentionally prioritizing exercise, nutrition, sleep, and stress management, you will be well-positioned to navigate the demands of creating your Encore Career, achieve overall well-being, and sustain a sense of harmony between work and life.

Pursuing Hobbies and Passions

As part of your semi-retirement plan, perhaps you intend to pursue new hobbies and passions, or carve out time to pick up past hobbies and passions you previously had to put aside earlier in your life. Whether you are reigniting your interests or identifying new ones, dedicating time to activities that bring you joy and relaxation are all part of creating your Encore Career and achieving work life harmony. Pursuing hobbies not only enhances your overall wellbeing and can reduce stress, but they can also serve as a source of creativity and inspiration for your Encore Career.

Pursuing hobbies and passions during your Encore Career can bring joy, a sense of fulfillment, and emphasize a purpose to your life. Reflect on activities or interests that ignite your curiosity, creativity, and sense of adventure. These could be hobbies you've enjoyed throughout your life or new interests you've always wanted to explore.

- Create a Plan: Once you've identified your passions, create a plan for incorporating them into your Encore Career. Determine how much time and resources you can dedicate to pursuing your hobbies and interests while balancing other commitments. If you thrive in structure, you may want to set specific goals, create a plan, and establish milestones to guide your progress. If you get your energy by engaging with others, consider undertaking the hobby along with others who have similar interests.
- Allocate Time: Prioritize your hobbies by allocating dedicated time in your schedule. Treat your hobbies with the same level of importance as your professional responsibilities. Whether it's painting, gardening, playing a musical instrument, practicing photography, or volunteering with a local youth group, schedule regular time for your chosen activities.
- Explore New Opportunities: Perhaps you want to use this time to explore new hobbies and interests. This may entail taking classes, attending workshops, or joining clubs related to your passions to expand your knowledge and skills. Embrace the spirit of curiosity and experimentation as you discover new activities that bring you joy. If you find that these new activities are not what you expected, you can choose to discontinue them - be sure to minimize any financial or time obligations you may have committed to.
- Combine Passion with Purpose: Consider how you can align your hobbies and passions with meaningful goals or causes. For example, if you enjoy painting, you could volunteer to teach art classes or use your artwork to raise awareness for social issues. Combining passion with purpose can amplify the impact of your activities.
- Connect with Like-Minded Individuals: Surround yourself with a community of individuals who share your interests

and passions. Join clubs, online forums, or local meetups where you can connect with like-minded individuals, share experiences, and learn from each other. Building a supportive network can enhance your enjoyment of your hobbies and provide valuable opportunities for growth and collaboration. You are also more likely to stay committed when you are connected with others.

- Embrace Creativity: Use your hobbies as a creative outlet to express yourself and explore new ideas. Whether you're writing poetry, designing jewelry, or experimenting with culinary creations, allow yourself the freedom to express your creativity without judgment or expectation. Embracing creativity can foster personal growth, self-discovery, and a deeper connection to your passions.
- Manage Your Time: Pursuing hobbies and passions is essential for overall well-being, but be mindful of not overcommitting yourself or neglecting other areas of your life. Remember the importance of nurturing relationships, maintaining your health, and ensuring time for your Encore Career responsibilities. Strive to strike a harmonious balance that allows you to enjoy your hobbies while finding fulfillment in the other parts of your life.
- Celebrate and Appreciate: you should feel fantastic about pursuing your hobbies and interests. Celebrate and appreciate what you are able to accomplish. Acknowledge any limitations and focus on the joy and fulfillment that these activities bring to your life. Appreciate the growth and learning you experience along the way.

In summary, Chapter 11 has reinforced the importance of achieving and maintaining a healthy and harmonious balance of work and life during your third act. As you navigate your Encore Career, you may find it useful to follow some of the suggested practical strategies for effective time management, staying physically and emotionally healthy, nurturing your personal relationships, and pursuing hobbies and passions. By mastering the principles outlined in this chapter, you can ensure that your Encore Career will be professionally rewarding as well as personally fulfilling and sustainable.

CHAPTER 12
Sustaining and Thriving in Your Third Act.

"If you look at what you have in life, you'll always have more.
If you look at what you don't have in life, you'll never have enough."
—Oprah Winfrey

Your Encore Career is an ongoing journey, and how you define a successful Encore Career as well as plan for your exit to full retirement may very well be unique to your journey. This chapter wraps it all up while exploring strategies for long-term success, reflecting on your Encore Career journey, and leaving behind a positive impact during and after your Encore Career.

Throughout this book, you have been thinking of all the ingredients you need for planning your successful Encore Career. This book has provided you with many ways to create your plan. You might be thinking about starting your Encore Career right away, or for some of you the start might begin in a few years. Whatever you decide, achieving success requires ongoing dedication and commitment, being open to personal and professional growth, and allowing yourself to evolve, adapt, and transform.

This Is About You

You are designing *where*, *when*, and *how* you will thrive in your third act. You have the choices in your Encore Career, and you are in control. To ensure you continue to thrive in your Encore Career, consider:

- What type of environments have I been successful in the past? Why was I successful?
- What type of environment do I need around me in order to continue to thrive in my Encore Career?
- What resources are available to me? How can I leverage these resources effectively and efficiently?

Getting here has already been a lifelong journey! Getting to this point in your life, where you are considering your Encore Career, has already been an adventure likely full of ups and downs, highs and lows. Every experience, skill, and aspect of knowledge that you have attained and retained along the way is part of who you are, they are the building blocks for whom you will be in your Encore Career.

You have already taken steps to invest in your success just by getting this far in our journey together. You have already recognized that your Encore Career endeavor required a commitment to growth, that's why you chose to go through this book. We encourage you to continue to invest in yourself, continue learning, and adapting to changing circumstances. Each experience that you have along the way of establishing, launching, and pursuing your Encore Career is a growth opportunity. Seeing this as a continuous process of learning and embracing the changes you are experiencing is essential for success - because change isn't always easy and sometimes requires more time, resources, and investments than we initially expected.

Be sure to give yourself some grace. View mistakes and successes as learning opportunities (what went well, and what didn't?) You will come away from experiences even stronger than before. Any journey and transformation is likely to have unexpected challenges and setbacks. Building resilience is essential for overcoming them. Using the strategies we've laid out will help you plan for the tactics of your Encore Career. Developing your personal resilience, such as maintaining a positive mindset, seeking support, and learning from adversity are foundational to being successful with these tactics.

Reflect on Your Journey

As you progress in launching and thriving in your Encore Career, your goals and priorities may evolve. We recommend that you periodically "check-in" with yourself. Evaluate where you are in your Encore Career journey. Ask yourself if this path is still working for you? Is it still aligned well with who I am and what I wish to spend my time on? It is okay to make adjustments as needed.

We encourage you to be flexible and open to new opportunities that align even better with your changing interests and values. You will likely be exposed to new ways of thinking, working, and interests simply by the nature of your interactions with new people in your Encore Career.

Seek out and find ongoing fulfillment. During your Encore Career it is important to think beyond supplementing your financial stability. While it may serve that purpose, if you are not continually finding fulfillment and purpose in your work, it may be time to reevaluate. As a gentle reminder, you embarked on your Encore Career to discover your purpose, identify what brings you joy and satisfaction, and to incorporate these elements into your Encore Career. This focus on fulfillment contributes to long-term happiness and motivation. Let's ensure you are keeping this top of mind. Ask yourself if you are feeling fulfilled and are you excited to talk with others about what you are doing? If the answer is yes, keep on doing it. If the answer is unclear or no, it is time to reevaluate your direction.

Perhaps you anticipated that starting your own business or taking on philanthropic efforts were going to leave a legacy. We encourage you to periodically reflect on what mark you wish to leave on those in your field, your community, or the world at large. Recognizing the potential for a meaningful legacy can be a powerful motivator for long-term success. You may have also considered that you want to prepare for others to continue your work. What are you doing now to ensure that your effort lasts? How can you establish a legacy that continues to live on? Are there family members you'd like to engage in your endeavors? Are there companies that would like to acquire what you've built? When you are ready to 'hand-over' the reins, to whom will you hand them to?

Sustaining and thriving in your Encore Career means putting yourself first, emphasizing what enables and allows you to thrive, reinforcing your commitment to both personal and professional growth, building personal resilience, periodically reevaluating your path, and aligning/realigning your efforts to ensure continued fulfillment. If you decide that you want to leave a legacy and ensure a certain impact you have to have a plan on how that will occur - don't leave it up to chance. You will continue to grow, adapt, and evolve. Having a compass for navigating the fulfilling journey of an Encore Career can help.

Embrace Lifelong Learning

Lifelong learning is a key element of thriving in your Encore Career. Having a growth mindset and being open to learning new information, different approaches, and adding new skills helps you stay cerebrally healthy, which is almost as important as staying physically healthy.

Building and maintaining strong connections with others is a key to living a life of learning. And speaking of health, according to the Center for Disease Control (CDC), people with strong social bonds have a 50% higher likelihood of staying healthy and preventing serious illnesses such as heart disease, stroke, dementia, depression, and anxiety. Having meaningful social connections is also linked to healthy habits such as eating well, sleeping well, and making the effort to experience an overall higher quality of life. Whether it is keeping up with your professional network, maintaining connection to your family members, or engaging with people in your community, connection is important.

We encourage you to also continue finding ways to improve and develop yourself. Periodic self-assessment and also getting feedback from others can help you continue to identify areas where you can grow. Developing yourself as you thrive in your Encore Career may include things like staying current with industry trends, completing courses on topics that interest you, picking up new hobbies, perhaps traveling to new places - all of these are diverse learning opportunities. They can also be opportunities for further networking and continuing to meet new people, which will further enhance your social connections and help you remain relevant and fulfilled in your Encore Career.

Prioritize Well-Being

Your personal well-being is paramount for thriving in your Encore Career. Consider how you will prioritize your health - physically, mentally, and emotionally - as an essential component of sustaining and thriving in your Encore Career. The ongoing nature of this effort, the prioritization of well-being, requires your attention to how you spend your time (time management), creating a conducive work-life environment, your ability to handle stress and personal resiliency, nurturing social connections and relationships, pursuing hobbies and passions that bring you joy, and remaining flexible and adaptable as things will always change in some way. With these in mind, you can ensure that your third act is not only professionally successful but also personally fulfilling and joyful.

What You Can Do For Others

Yes, we just got finished saying it has been all about you, but don't forget that you chose your Encore Career direction because it was aligned with your passions and interests. Therefore, it is highly likely that you chose a direction that would have a positive impact on others. You may choose to continue paying it forward by becoming a mentor to others. Perhaps you will choose to mentor those who are earlier in their career, and you will choose to share your knowledge and expertise generously. Alternatively, you may have acquired a new skill and wish to share it with others in your professional network.

As you find success in your Encore Career, share your learnings from this journey with others who are just considering how to start their own Encore Career. Both your successes and your failures have been opportunities for learning. Reflecting on any setbacks you experienced can become 'pitfalls to avoid' lessons for others as you share your experiences. Understanding what went wrong and what you would do differently now can be instrumental for others to avoid similar challenges and make better-informed decisions.

Helping others to build their own personal resilience can be a very valuable use of your time. Sharing some of the strategies for building resilience from this book might be a way to get started. Some of these strategies to become more resilient included: maintaining a positive outlook, seeking support from others, building a network, and practicing self-compassion. Resilience helps people overcome difficult challenges and setbacks, navigate through times of transition, and empowers people to bounce back from disappointments and continue their journey with determination. Your mentoring can be a great service to them.

The Legacy of Your Encore Career

By sharing your story and your wisdom, you encourage and empower others to embark on their Encore Careers with enthusiasm, resilience, and purpose. Your Encore Career is not just about the work you will do or the goals you will have achieved - it can also be about the legacy you build and what lasting impact you want to have. As a professional, you've contributed your skills, experience, and passions to your chosen field, leaving a lasting impact. Perhaps you've mentored others, given back to your community, and made a difference in people's lives. Or perhaps during your primary career you didn't have time to do these things even though you wanted to. Your Encore Career legacy can be a start or continuation of these contributions as well as a reflection of your values, your growth, and your commitment to a life well-lived.

An Encore Career is not just about personal fulfillment but can also be about making a meaningful impact on the world. Are you leaving a legacy? Are you giving back to society? Whether through mentorship, volunteering, philanthropy, or other forms of contribution, you can make a meaningful difference.

Embrace the Future with Enthusiasm

As you look forward to the future, remember that your journey is far from over. You have the power to continue shaping your Encore Career, embracing new opportunities, and adapting to change. Your potential for growth and personal fulfillment is boundless. Approach this phase of your life with the same enthusiasm and curiosity that have carried you this far.

Words of Encouragement

To those of you who will now embark on creating your Encore Careers, we offer these words of encouragement:

- Embrace change as a catalyst for growth and self-discovery.
- Be open to learning, remain adaptable, and view setbacks as stepping stones to success.
- Seek balance in your work and life, nurturing your well-being and relationships.

- Make a positive impact on your community and the world, leaving a meaningful legacy.
- Most importantly, pursue your passions and interests with unwavering dedication and enthusiasm.

Your Encore Career is not a destination but a journey. It's an opportunity to explore your passions, make a difference, and continue evolving as an individual. As you move forward, remember that the best could be yet to come. Be an inspiration to others and show gratitude to those around you who have been an inspiration to you.

In summary, Chapter 12 is a guide to sustaining and thriving in the long term within an Encore Career. It provides you with strategies for thriving in your Encore Career and beyond. By mastering the principles outlined in this chapter, you can build and sustain an Encore Career that is a source of satisfaction, purpose, and success throughout the remainder of your working journey.

* * * *

In closing, we celebrate you, your Encore Career journey, and the legacy you're creating. We look forward to the continued impact you'll make, and we're excited to see where your path leads you. Your Encore Career is a testament to the potential for growth, fulfillment, and purpose at any stage of life. May it inspire you and others to embrace your unique third act with open hearts and open minds.

APPENDIX
Additional Resources

Below is a list of various additional resources, including books, websites, and organizations that can provide further guidance and support to you as you pursue your Encore Career.

For information on how to establish Encore Career coaching with MPrince Consulting LLC, visit MPrince Consulting LLC on LinkedIn.

Resources referenced in this book:

Introduction

https://www.ted.com/talks/jane_fonda_life_s_third_act
"The 100-year Life: Living and Working in and Age of Longevity"

Chapter 1

Redesigning Retirement
How state-mandated retirement plans work
www.sba.gov Small Business Administration, government resources.
www.Salary.com to ensure you know what you are worth. This site provides pay, bonus, and benefits information for jobs (filter by level, geographic location, years of experience, etc.)

Chapter 2

Self-reflection Assessments

The idea of a career change in your Encore Career can be overwhelming. Here are some self-assessment tools that can help you to better understand your natural style and preferences, and analyze what some of your third act interests might be. A small fee might be associated with obtaining the results.

- Career Aptitude Test
- Myers Briggs Type Indicator (MBTI)
- Enneagram Personality Test

- O*NET Interest Profiler
- This site has numerous assessments to choose from

Chapter 3

Resources for Flexible Professional Jobs – flexjobs.com, fiverr.com, aarp.com, LinkedIn.com networking/groups, Facebook groups, your own alumni resources, and your own network.
Maximize the Silver workforce
Gemini/AI - can help you identify a career path (enter your education, skills, experience, desires, motivations) and ask it to identify ideal career moves for you.

Chapter 4

Strategies for Building Resilience
How Women Rise by Sally Helgesen

Chapter 5

How Do I Create a Good LinkedIn Profile?
Best Website Builders 2024

Chapter 6

Financial planning resources: This is Pretirement
Your Medicare choices

Chapter 7

Upskilling post-50 and why and how to do it

Chapter 8

Small business expert tips and insights for older entrepreneurs on starting a small business and running it successfully.

Business Plan Models:
https://www.strategyzer.com/library/business-models Ideal for the more left-brained people.
https://www.rightbrainbusinessplan.com/ Ideal for the more creative-type people.

Chapter 9

See the Job Boards referenced in the chapter.
AARP.org/work & jobs section has resources tailored to Encore Careers and age-friendly workplaces.

Chapter 10

The Neuroscience of Gratitude and Effects on the Brain

Chapter 11

Eisenhower Matrix for Time Management https://www.eisenhower.me/eisenhower-matrix

Chapter 12

Health Benefits of Social Connectedness
Maintaining Your Brain Health

Made in the USA
Columbia, SC
09 July 2024

fae92d14-009b-458d-8a02-5c30ae4a4f54R02